THEN GOD STEPPED IN

THEN GOD STEPPED IN

Testimonies of the Lord's Deliverances

by

WORLDWIDE EVANGELIZATION CRUSADERS

Edited by

LEONARD C. J. MOULES

CHRISTIAN LITERATURE CRUSADE

LONDON

CHRISTIAN LITERATURE CRUSADE
The Dean, Alresford, Hants

First Published 1963
Reprinted 1964, 1966, 1973

SBN 900284 20X

Printed in Great Britain by Richard Clay (The Chaucer Press), Ltd.
Bungay, Suffolk

CONTENTS

INTRODUCTION

THIS book is a testimony and only a testimony. Throughout the years God's faithfulness to us has been confirmed. The time is long overdue for us to give Him the glory and praise due to His name.

Then God Stepped In is a record of His presence in both ordinary and outstanding circumstances. But it is by no means complete, for we find that God is daily "stepping in" to our affairs. He is sovereign to rule our lives and order our work. He must step in. In the testimonies which follow you will read repeatedly the expression that God is in our "stops" as well as in our "starts" and "steps". Paul would have used this expression had he been relating his intentions about Bithynia to us today.

Here is the same thought written by Peggy Easton of Colombia. She who has known the fires of persecution can well write: "Few are the Christians who cannot recall occasions when God in timely and remarkable ways has come to their aid in sovereign power. At such times as these He has 'moved the stone', made the 'mountain a way', opened blind eyes to see His Hosts, or provided the very thing that was lacking. Sometimes He has revealed Himself in the midst of a spiritual battle when all seemed lost. He has dealt in judgement with the adversary when Satan was ready to pounce on the prey. Have we not seen him in control as Captain of the Host of the Lord turning danger to safety and darkness to light, fear into faith and despair to buoyant hope."

Every servant of God finds himself in extremities—at "wit's end" as the Psalmist calls it. We are there either because it pleases God in this way to reveal Himself more fully, or, as is often the case, because foolish reasoning and wilful independence have lured us to such an extremity. Whatever the reason may be, if out of this darkness there is a cry to God for help or intervention then He, in His richness of mercy, steps in. The scene is changed! Everything comes into its rightful place and perfect harmony is created.

We would be much the poorer without these experiences, and who can rob us of the precious things we learn from these lessons on life's shaded and shadowy pages.

Steve Jacobs of India emphasizes the practicality of God's presence as against the spirituality of His promise. Here is a quotation from his letter, "For the midday meal my wife placed a dish of *dhal* (lentils) on the table. I bowed my head for grace and gave thanks, 'Lord, you know how I loathe this *dhal*, but you blessed this same food to your servant Daniel and his three companions. They thrived on it more than those who ate luxuries at the king's table. Likewise, Lord, bless it to us for Thy name's sake. Amen.' I ate with relish. I told my wife it was one of the nicest meals I had ever eaten." God had stepped in.

"One day the typewriter cast a type—and of all the letters it would be the 'a': my fountain pen was now the only medium of writing, and by it to reach thousands of hungry souls with our Bible correspondence courses. The nib broke. With no replacement, or facility to get a new nib, I prayed in this predicament. I remembered a piece of thin bamboo on the shelf. With a great deal of sweat and patience I shaped a nib. With this old-fashioned instrument the ministry continued. But I wrote with depression. I was rebellious. Here was I trying to reach thousands with the Good News of Salvation, and I could not even afford a pen-nib. God said to me, 'My son, My Holy Word was written by My servants with pens just like yours.' I replied, 'Thank you, Lord, that better men than I have written better words with pens such as this one. Amen.' God had stepped in."

This testimony of the Crusade is commended to you that its reading may make you aware that God wants to step into your life in both its insignificant but important detail and in its crises.

L. C. J. Moules

A DOXOLOGY IN SMOKE

"Neither shall the flame kindle upon thee"
Isaiah 43: 2.

IRIS MOULES *India*

"THIS is the only town I know that is built on a precipice"—a comment upon Mussoorie, the hill station of India, by a well-known American Christian leader. A 7,000-ft. ridge holds the town of no small importance as a disused military centre and summer resort for Rajahs and Government officials. The Eastern sector—the highest—is in the main the venue of missionary personnel coming and going from April to September, seeking a snatched respite from the fierce heat of the Plains.

"Jesscot" was built precariously near the summit. It looked a simple jump from the verandah into the falling depths below. The actual steepness was broken by the woods of rhododendron and fir trees which clung tenaciously to the hillside. The branches of the trees touched the bungalow as the winds moaned through and up the wooded slopes.

This was the centre for our missionary candidates studying the language. The School was on the very summit. Fifteen or more recruits from our various National Headquarters formed a dedicated group of young life adjusting itself to the orientation of a new life and country.

Weird sounds disturbed the stillness of the woods as language teachers giving private studies put the students through their phonetic drill. Others waited or studied on the concrete walk on two sides of the bungalow. This was a vantage point that commanded a distant view over hills and valleys. Visibility today was limited by the smoky and heavy atmosphere. Forest fires were attracting attention by the palls of smoke.

Our attention became more and more fixed on what we called the "dhobie ghat" (washerman's pool), where a cluster of houses by the river located the caste that handled the laundrywork. The wisp of smoke mushroomed and billowed into a thickening fog. It crept up to us through branches. Figures could be seen hurrying up a narrow zig-zagging path. Soon a caterpillar of human life, clutching all it could possibly carry, slowly moved to escape from the tragedy engulfing them.

We were too engrossed to notice the further arrival of language teachers. A comment from one of them reminded us that language was a priority even if our clothes were being burnt in the laundry three miles away down the mountainside! Our move to lessons was halted by a cry, "It's right here! Look!" An ominous crackle of the burning undergrowth increased as it raced up to the bungalow. Looking far distant, we had failed to spot a new source of fire through a spark. Our immediate hillside was threatened with real danger.

Neighbours saw our predicament and raced along the narrow mountain path to our aid. They tried to cut a fire break. Water was the only counter-weapon to hand, but the distance we were from the water tower never allowed us to have but a trickle. It now mocked us as we waited for buckets to fill. We wanted to close our ears to the sound and think what we would take if evacuation were finally enforced.

The atmosphere choked us. Visibility—nil! The wind urged on the fire to complete its devastation. The metal handrail around the verandah became too hot to touch. Grass tufts at our feet burned out. A large tree partially overhanging the roof was well in flame near the wooden joists and beams. Terror appeared on the face of a screaming five-year-old. An expectant mother becoming greatly agitated confirmed the wisdom for some to join the retreat along and up the narrow wooded path. Refuge in a higher neighbouring home was a possibility.

Great as the united effort was, it was not enough. The forest fire gained in spite of it all. While heroic efforts by the men were maintained, a few of us who could only watch anyway, gathered at the rear of the house. We cast ourselves upon God. We handed the situation to Him. Inside the house a sick candidate lay in bed. He remained confident and unmoved! He had more faith than we had, but we had an assurance that God would not leave us. This confidence rapidly grew, and we thanked Him! Then prayer was overtoned by a deep rumble of thunder. A spot of rain dashed on the cheek. Then came a roar as the downpour crashed on to the hot corrugated iron roof. The wind suddenly veered right about, and the fire was forced back on itself. The flames died quickly and the smouldering forest gently hissed in the drenching rain.

"Hath the rain a father?" asked Job. There could be no doubt our God is a God of the elements who promises that the flame shall not kindle upon us.

God again preserved life when a babe was born prematurely to its mother. The excitement and apprehension had taken its natural course within the bounds of His loving Hand.

BEDROLLS AND BIBLES

"I will satisfy Him" Psalm 91:16.

JOCK PURVES *N.W. Frontier, India (now Pakistan)*

How often we looked across the border! Many a time we could have walked across! There were days when at the far end of the Khyber Pass we leaned on the bar of the Frontier gate and gazed into the forbidden land of Afghanistan. The sentries stood silent at their posts. On the rocks above soldiers of the Indian Army watched us from behind their machine guns.

It was of no use to go over. At best we would have been arrested and handed back to the British Government, and at worst we might have been shot. Such an act as crossing the border would in no wise have aided missionary work. We would have been asked to leave the area, and be farther from the border than ever. We applied to the British Commissioner to live nearer the border. The answer was a large sheet of white paper with but a few lines on it assuring us that there could be no change of residence!

There were four of us at that time in Kohat: two ladies, one British and the other a Dane actually living in the city itself, while the two men, one British and the other American, lived outside the city gates and barbed-wire entanglements. Day and night we worked in the city. To enter we had to knock at the small postern gate set in the main city gates. We were always answered by a challenge from the sentries.

The church on the hill was built by ourselves. Its white dome fell in the first time we put it up. I was in charge of the open air work. The devil put me through the mill every time I was due to lead it. There was no one to lead but myself, and nobody came for the prayer session before the open air meeting.

After prayer alone I set off for a stand not far from the main city gate. Not many were around until I began to read aloud the Word of God. Very soon I would be hemmed in by a boisterous but listening crowd. Questions would come shooting swiftly from many directions, with little time to answer each one adequately. "Do you drink wine?" I would answer reassuringly, "No!" The next inevitably followed, "Do you eat pig?" Again would come the reassuring "No." (I did not because they did not. Better to have no debates about that.) "Oh, then you're nearly a Moslem!" "Well, you may think so, but listen to this." I would open my Bible and read the words of the Saviour showing that not what goes into a man's stomach but what comes out of his heart defiles him. Brows would knit, there would be scowls and mutterings. Other questions would reach me, some angry, some framed to create laughter. Suddenly a cry would be raised. "God is great! There is no God but one God, and Mohamed is His prophet!" I stood silent. One of their number would begin to address the crowd. I would appeal, and say smilingly, "This is my meeting." They would laugh and taunt, "Oh no, it isn't! Not now. You're free to ask any questions if you want to." But sometimes it was nasty as a stone caught me in the back. A humble Christian would shadow me all the way home, watching sympathetically. Later I would be warned by him of impending dangers. Sometimes the crowd surged towards me with wild cries as we were forced up the street. The police then drew their batons, hitting in front of us right and left. Open-air preaching was not a good method. We changed from it to more profitable personal work, but ever our hearts were over the border.

We all four applied to go to Kabul for a month as tourists! We Britishers were soon dealt with! I was called before an official and told that to go to Kabul I needed a personal invitation from the British Ambassador. But the American and the Dane were given permission for a month in Kabul! Wonderful!

Donald and I got to work. We invented a language in code. Our letters to each other would be read by Afghan officials. There would be very little about the Son of God and His missionary work written in them.

"The roses round the door" would mean "The national Christians beside me!" Then Donald made a will. He left me a bit in case he did not return.

But why was he going? He was going to see the land and its needs, and to find out if there was any possibility at all of opening a Christian dispensary in Kabul. Then again, why not take a great number of Scriptures in Arabic, Pushto and Persian? But how? The Afghan Government would never permit them to be read by their people. At least one main Customs post would have to be passed entering Kabul. The baggage would be examined and they would be confiscated. Donald and his companion would be sent out of the country. We prayed, and were particularly led to get the New Testaments and Gospels into Kabul, the very capital of Afghanistan.

Where could we put them? Donald would be taking his bedroll and blankets. A bright idea! Out were spread the blankets and in between each two were lined the Scriptures layer by layer. We rolled the blankets up, slid them into the bedroll, then tried to lift it. I laughed until the tears ran down my cheeks! Donald sat solemnly looking at me as if I had lost my reason! "Why all the laughter?" he asked. "Why," I said, "these are the heaviest blankets I've ever known, and the people at the Customs post will say the same." He breathed deeply as he tried to lift the bedroll. "This is no laughing matter," he grunted.

We talked and thought and prayed. The Scriptures must go! And go they did. Next day we set off for the Khyber Pass to give them a hand with their luggage. I saw them move under the frontier pole into the closed land of Afghanistan.

Only a few letters passed between us. Rioting with assassinations and war broke out in the land. European nationals were taken out by air. Weeks passed without a word of our two friends. The wild borders now became restless, and we wondered if the fighting would reach us.

Then one day Donald was hammering at my door. "Let me in quickly," he said. "I think all the newspaper reporters in India are at my heels. I can't stay many days with you. You too should move. Things are critical." Later he gave me his story, and it was one of daring and danger for our Danish sister and for him. "What of the Scriptures?" I asked. "Oh, wonderful," he said. "I got each New Testament and Gospel away personally into the hands of an Afghan reader. God has marvellously answered prayer. We got every one into Kabul!"

This is how God had stepped in. It appeared that while on their way to the capital over a difficult camel track, the car broke down not too far from Kabul. They sat on the rocks while the driver grumblingly did what he could but told them coldly that he could go no farther. They waited for the Lord's deliverance, and it came. As darkness was falling a horse ambled by drawing a two-wheeled cart. Would the driver take them to Kabul? Yes, if they paid. They would pay all right! Off came the various bundles and bedrolls from the car, and the cart was loaded up. They tumbled in after them, and in the darkness slowly made for Kabul. They told the driver where they wished to go in the city, and he took them by a direct route. But what of the Customs post and what happened there? Well, nothing, for the driver of the *tonga* just never thought about Customs posts and knew his own way into the city, not by the main route at all. "There the heaviest blankets I've ever come across were dumped right in the heart of the closed land," said Donald. "Each Bible and Gospel was given to a known Afghan reader." God had stepped in and stayed until our fellow-missionaries were safely with us again.

A SUMMER OF SUFFERING

"*A thousand shall fall at thy side*" Psalm 91: 7.

LILY BOAL *Kashmir*

IN the year 1947 India was at last to get her long-claimed Independence. At the same time, the Moslems of the sub-continent were to have their own separate State. We could not believe that this would involve our beautiful Kashmir in trouble! All through the War years we had been free to carry on the work of the Gospel without hindrance.

That very summer Margaret Brown and I had been led to open a new mission station in Buniyar, in the Jhelum Valley in Kashmir. A number of orphan children, who had been in my care as babies, were with us. Three were attending the Central Asian Mission School in Bandipur. We also had with us an older orphan girl who helped us in the home, and Miriam, the mother of one of the children, a dear Christian woman. We operated a dispensary for the village people by means of which we were making contacts with them.

This was the situation in which we were quietly working when the tribesmen of the Frontier began gathering (unknown to us) to "liberate" their Moslem brethren of Kashmir, whose ruler had seceded to the new India! Although we did hear rumours of trouble down-country, we still did not believe it would come to Kashmir. I was then preparing for furlough and decided to take a trip to Srinagar, the capital of Kashmir, to do my final shopping and bid farewell to both Indian and missionary friends.

It was almost impossible to get transport of any kind to take me to Srinagar. Eventually I was able to ride in a *tonga* as far as Baramulla, and continued on to Srinagar by bus. In Baramulla, people were talking a good deal of events in the Punjab and of the tribesmen's threat to come up to Srinagar. In the capital I stayed some days in the Church Missionary Society hospital. More rumours reached us till I became really alarmed. I sent Margaret a wire that I was returning to the station. At that very hour the tribesmen were entering Kashmir. Thousands of people were fleeing before them, while others not quick enough in making their escape were cruelly murdered.

The Lord's command to me had been, "Occupy till I come". I felt it was my duty to return. I spent the afternoon anxiously trying to get transport by road to Buniyar, but was unsuccessful. Then I met a Kashmiri boatman whom I knew, and told him of my difficulty. He was amazed and said, "Miss Sahib, the tribesmen are now on their way up the valley and it is far too dangerous for you to attempt to go!" But finally, seeing my desperation to get back to my friends, this man agreed to take me down the river in his boat. He arranged to start at dusk, about five in the evening. The missionaries at the hospital, on hearing this plan, did their best to dissuade me, especially one Sister who was very distressed at my going.

As night fell I embarked. Although the distance to Baramulla is only about forty miles, it seemed a long, slow, and anxious journey. We travelled all night, because the raiders were now all over the country and it was too risky to travel by daylight. At Baramulla we faced the unforgettable sight of hundreds of men, women, and children, mostly Sikhs, carrying a few possessions in bundles on their heads, fleeing from the advancing raiders. Leaving the boat and accompanied by the faithful boatman, I looked for transport and found a *tonga-walla* (driver of a sort of horse and trap), who was astonished by my asking him to take me the fourteen miles back to our station in Buniyar. He said, looking me right in the face, "Miss Sahib, if you were to offer me one thousand rupees, I would not take you one step on that journey!" Then he added, "Run somewhere to safety, or you will be murdered!" The Roman Catholic Hospital was near, and standing in the gateway was a nun. I asked her about the situation and told her that I was trying to get through to Buniyar. She begged me not to attempt to go farther. Taking me in, she led me to a tiny room in which three Hindu girls had already taken refuge. The Superintending Sister asked if I would take these young girls "under my wing", as they were naturally very frightened indeed. In that little room I had the precious opportunity of speaking to those girls about the Saviour's love for them.

Among the crowd of some 100 people who were gathered in the hospital was Colonel Dykes with his wife and three children, the youngest of whom had been born in the hospital and was only twelve days old! We became friendly and the Colonel joked about the Frontier "where there ain't no Ten Commandments". He tried to encourage us all by saying that the hospital was so well known that the tribesmen would not molest them.

In the evening of Saturday, 25th October, the tribesmen reached Baramulla bazaar. They were looting and killing. The bazaar is only ten minutes' walk from the hospital, so this was a somewhat terrifying piece of news. Everyone was anxious and upset, yet the Lord enabled me to lie down in peaceful sleep that night. Early in the morning a knock came at my door, and the Mother Superior entered bringing me a cup of tea. She looked worried when she said, "Miss Boal, I am afraid we are in for serious trouble today. The tribesmen have looted and burned the bazaar, and murdered many people." I replied that we must all pray, as God alone was able to deliver us. Who was to know that the Mother Superior herself would be the first woman in the hospital to be shot?

After a while, Colonel Dykes, his wife and I began to walk up and down the hospital compound together. The Colonel was still full of fun and jokes about the Pathans, and was no doubt trying to keep up our morale. Even then, we could hear the sounds of shooting and people screaming, and we women thought it wise to return to our rooms. With wild shouts the Pathans arrived, leaping over the compound walls.

Quickly I gathered the three frightened young Hindu girls together, and sought to prepare them should we be suddenly called from this world. Then I fell on my knees and my heart cried out to God. I had little faith for my own deliverance. Death appeared to be certain. I prayed for my loved ones; my fellow workers and all our Indian women and children dear to me. As I prayed, I heard the terrible cries of people being murdered! We listened fearfully to the tribesmen striding through the rooms and banging on the doors. The shouting and footsteps came nearer to us! Then they were next door in the operating theatre wantonly destroying what was of no use to them as loot. At last the Pathans were banging on our barred door. The girls were terrified and begged me not to open it. We felt death preferable to something which we knew would be worse.

Quietly we retreated from our room into the adjoining bathroom, bolting the doors behind us. We had barely hidden ourselves when the Pathans broke into the room we had vacated, and were evidently looting all our stuff. It would have been death for us to have remained in that room. The bathroom door shuddered under the banging as the men demanded admission. I flung open the door and was faced with an armed Pathan. He aimed the rifle at me! I cried in Urdu, "Long live Pakistan!" and at once he dropped his gun, saying fiercely, "Then give me your money!" I calmly replied, "You have already had it." "Come outside!" he yelled, and we felt our last moments had come. We stumbled out only to find that the man had disappeared. There was only one answer to this—God had delivered us!

I ran to the front of the hospital to be with the rest of the people, and to see how they were faring. What a terrible sight met my eyes! Two nuns, covered with blood, lay dying. The children of Colonel Dykes were wandering about alone. On seeing me, the Colonel's servant cried out, "Oh, Miss Sahib, thank God you are safe. He has spared you. Come and see the Colonel, for he has been shot." I knelt by the officer now lying on the verandah and bleeding freely. I managed somehow to drag him inside his room and on to the bed. I cannot imagine how I did it, for he was a tall well-built man about thirty-five years of age. His wife had been shot dead, and her body was found later down the well where the tribesmen had flung it. The Colonel died a few hours later. The Mother Superior's condition was also serious, for she had been shot with five or six others.

After this terrible assault, we who survived remained for thirteen days in a small babies' ward. We had to wait for our rescue. The Pathans held life cheaply, and one day, seeing my watch, one came up, pointed his gun-barrel at me, and demanded it. Some urged, "Miss Boal, don't give it up." I replied, "Then we'll be murdered." I slipped the watch off my wrist and handed it to him. One old woman did not take her ring off fast enough, so angrily they slashed her finger off.

While I tried to help the Colonel in his dying minutes, he asked, "Miss Boal, where are my wife and children?" "You must not worry about your children," I replied, "I will look after them." Raising himself up, he looked over to the cot behind the door, and, following his gaze, I discovered baby James lying there. I lifted the poor motherless child into my arms and looked for something to wrap him in. Alas, everything had been looted. In the bathroom I found a towel, and, wrapping it around him, took him out into the compound where the Colonel's two boys were wandering. They ran up to me and said, "Oh, you have got our little brother; we want to stay with you, too!" Thus I found myself in charge of these little ones so desperately in need of love and care.

The tribesmen continued their terrible activities. They lined up the surviving nuns, and wrenched from them their rings and crosses. They were just about to murder them, when the husband of the lady doctor stepped forward calling, "Kill me, and leave the Sisters alone!" They took him at his word.

A new contingent of Pathans arrived at the hospital. To us all it was a great relief to find they were not so wild as the previous ones. These were more disciplined as an army. The priests pleaded with them to do something for us all, in view of what we had passed through. They agreed that, if all the people (numbering about 100) would go into one room, they would put a guard on it, and see that no more atrocities were committed. We all crowded into one small ward.

One night I awoke to find the whole place aglow, and thought the hospital was on fire. However, it proved to be the nearby match factory. Other tribesmen had gone up the valley, and had actually reached the Srinagar airfield. There they were met in the nick of time by units of the Indian Army, who turned them back and pursued them down the valley. Indian planes now began to come over, and they started to drop bombs! This seemed to be the culmination of all the previous horrors! The more orderly Pathans dug trenches in the compound, and we ran out to hide in them. Thomas and Douglas Dykes thought this was fun, so I did my best not to enlighten them. I cannot tell how often we hid baby James under the bed. I did not really have faith in my heart for deliverance, and prayed only for grace to endure to the end.

A young man interned with us came in with the news that our own missionary, Ron Davis, had been killed, together with a faithful Christian woman, Miriam. He had heard also that our station had been looted and the orphan children were hiding in the jungle. The children were safe, but I did not know that until later.

We ventured more freely about the compound and were able to retrieve a few of our lost articles. I was delighted to find a tube of toothpaste which had been in my sponge bag. One of the girls showed me her "find"—a *Daily Light* which had been given her by a missionary. This she said I could have, and I received it as a great treasure. Thanking the girl for the *Daily Light*, I said, "We can all read it together." Through reading this I received, for the first time, a definite assurance that we would be delivered. We found nothing else of value. My coat and bedding had all been taken.

The Pathans were finally persuaded to allow the very seriously wounded to be taken down-country in a bus, and the gentleman who escorted them had previously informed the Government of our plight.

During the twelve days of captivity we received very little food, and were all weary of the close, uncomfortable quarters and the dangerous conditions. Then wonderful news came at last; the Pakistan Government was sending relief! We wept, laughed, clapped our hands and thankfully praised God. We waited through another long day to watch again the sun set over the Kashmir hills and mountains. Twilight had deepened to night before we heard the noise of a convoy of Army jeeps and trucks arrive. Quietly, yet quickly, we helped each other into the vehicles till all were crushed tightly inside. I remembered we must pass our station on our way, so asked, and received, permission to sit beside the driver of the first jeep. At the officer's request I threw a blanket around me so that I might not be recognized as a woman.

Tribesmen were still around so the officer commanding the rescue convoy waited until about 11 p.m. to drive quietly out of town without attracting their attention. But we were not successful, for almost immediately a group of blood-thirsty Pathans halted us. They were for murdering us all. Just in the nick of time, some of the more organized units came along and forced our captors to leave us alone. Eventually we got out of the town by a quiet roundabout route. It was a miraculous escape.

We reached Buniyar. Little did I guess that under the broken bridge we passed, lay the remains of Ron Davis.

He had been murdered in cold blood while trying to save others.

The Major consented to stop for a few minutes at Buniyar, and accompanied me the few yards to our house. It was deserted and looted. I wept, and after being led kindly back to the convoy, we proceeded down the valley. A thunderstorm echoed through the hills. The lightning showed up dead bodies on the roadside, and the rain poured down as though heaven wept with us. All around burned and ruined houses smouldered. As the dawn strengthened, the first rays of the sun lit up in welcome the refuge of Abbottabad. We were through.

A FROSTY HALLELUJAH

"He shall call upon me, and I will answer Him"
Psalm 91: 15.

LEN MOULES *Himalayan Field*

HE was a lone hurrying figure. As he twisted his way down the dusty shaly mountain-side I could see the plume of dust rise from each step. I was expecting him. Two weeks previously he had left me at our Mission post at Milam to climb the glaciers and take a message to the local Tibetan chief across the border. My desire was to enter the closed land of Tibet by accompanying the trade caravans to the markets of Gyanima, taking with me two yak-loads of Bibles. This approaching messenger bore the answer that was everything to me just then. To go—or not to go? I broke the seals and scanned the reply from the Indian Trade Agent in Gyanima, writing on behalf of the Tibetan chieftain. "I deeply regret . . ." I folded the letter, and, after expressing my profuse thanks to the courier and paying him well, turned dejectedly and went up the stone steps to my room. The one door by which I had hoped to enter that needy land had slammed in my face. How were the Tibetans ever to be reached with the Gospel?

"What's the matter, Sahib?" A Christian trading between Tibet and India posed the question, seeing my troubled face. I told him. "But I'll take them for you. It would be better so, for I know the customs and the language which you do not. I have travelled these high passes since boyhood—to you it is difficult and costly. I can give these sacred Scriptures and tell them what Christ means to me. I'll take them."

The personal disappointment was overwhelmed by joy at this amazing offer. Only God could have stepped in to prompt such an arrangement. So, for several years, the Tibetan Bibles went into this Forbidden Land. The faithful disciple led his yaks over 19,000-foot high passes to release the living Word into that land.

During those years the scene changed. In 1951 Tibet was forced to yield to Communist occupation. The passes from India to Tibet were manned at entrance and exit by police posts and Army units of both Governments. A radio post and police unit arrived in Milam. They were in direct contact with Delhi. Even my missionary activities were watched and interpreted into the Morse messages that were exchanged each night.

The radio operator saluted. He handed me a buff radiogram. The message was clear and to the point—no further consignments of religious literature were permitted to leave India for Tibet! I acknowledged receipt of the message. The operator saluted again, and, with a smart "about turn", hurried back to the post. They knew I had been an officer in the Army, and still accorded me full recognition in salutes!

Upstairs, I looked at the loads of Bibles piled against the wall. All were ready in weighed bundles for animal transport. In one week the passes would be open and the caravans would leave. In two weeks not a trader would be left in the valley. Only two weeks left! And the authority of the Government of India stood between those Bibles and Tibet. Who could we ask to step in on our behalf? Only God.

On my knees over the camp bed I bent in prayer and thought. Plans and prayers—prayers and plans! Only one plan was confirmed by His peace, and this was put into action. Air letters were sent to our International Home Bases to rally specific prayer support immediately. A further air letter went to my own prayer group through a very faithful friend in England. These air letters took four days' continual travel by mail runner through the mountains, and then a further three days by plane to reach their destinations. In fact, the trade with Tibet would have begun by the time the full volume of prayer could be expected. At the most, there would be only three days of worldwide prayer before the last trader left!

Day by day I watched the caravans leave. On Thursday only two remained. On Friday only one caravan was left, and that was due to depart before light on Saturday morning. Although busy with a thousand and one medical demands, my heart was continually at prayer, "Oh, God, only You can step in and release these Bibles. Lord God, Thy children worldwide are praying today. You have promised if only two agree. Can you refuse us?"

I even tried to "open the door" by pleading with the operator to convey a further request to Delhi. To him that buff form was the law of the Medes and Persians. Personally, he would like to—but he dared not. I returned to my room.

It was Friday night. Before the sun rose again, the last opportunity for the Bibles to go would have passed for another year. Frankly, I had little hope and less faith! But my spirit would not abandon the knowledge of a faithful God in hearing the prayers of His people, though this time, it seemed, it was not to be. Perhaps His denial is also His answer. I turned in, and was soon asleep.

"Sahib! Sahib!" I awoke. "Who's there?" "It's the radio post with a message for you, Sahib." Flashing my torch, I hurried down into the yard. The cold reminded me I was only in my pyjamas. Another buff envelope. They always seem to bring ominous news, and at this time of the night what next could it mean? I held the form in the torchlight, and read. I couldn't believe my eyes. The radio message merely cancelled the previous one to me! But this meant the Bibles could go. Into the frosty night I yelled a "Hallelujah!" The operator forgot his customary salute, and hurried away from the "mad" Englishman.

Upstairs I dressed warmly, and, armed with a big stick as defence against Tibetan dogs, hurried into the dark, silent, sleeping village. My knocking on the door awakened the trader, and the barking of the dogs awakened the village! Even now I wondered if the Bibles could be taken. What trader would have two unladen animals within hours of leaving for Tibet? Some might, but not our traders. Every animal carried every pound weight that it could manage. The door opened, and in my hurry I fell into the room. The trader, a good friend, laughed at my eager concern and rush. "Two spare animals for loads? Yes, I have two. I'm bringing back two loads more than I have on the outward journey. I will gladly take the Bibles and deliver them to H.S." (Our Christian trader had left the first day. He would be met at the markets.)

His sons and servants carried the Bible loads down to the animal lines. I did not sleep that night at all; I was so excited over God's outstanding mercy and grace to us all worldwide who had been praying. Little white puffs of breath in the cold atmosphere of the room registered a frequent "Hallelujah!"

It was about 4.30 a.m. Through the barred narrow

glassless window came the faint jingle of bells. The yaks were leaving the village. The last caravan was on its way. The Bibles were going over. God had stepped in.

In the morning I reached for an air form.

SAVED FROM THE SHYOK

"*But it shall not come nigh thee*" Psalm 91: 7.

JOCK PURVES *Lesser Tibet*

THE Karakoram, in the Western Himalaya, is a battleground of ice and snow for mountaineers. Here are the greatest glaciers outside of the Polar regions, fed by the mountain massifs of K2, Mt. Godwin Austen (28,250 feet above sea level), Rakaposhi (25,550 feet), and a thousand giant satellites. Sometimes in the movements of these mighty and colossal ice barriers, the valley they lead into is blocked by an ice wall hundreds of feet high. A natural ice-dam is formed and the rushing torrents from other ice systems build up behind it.

This happens at times near the source of the Shyok River where it rises in the high Karakoram. A lake fills cold and deep behind the ice-dam fingering up the snowy valley as far as twelve miles. The ice-barrier holds the pent-up torrents until the pressure becomes too great, then it snaps with the reverberating crash of a hundred thunders. Roaring and foaming, the destroying waters carry death and devastation as far as a thousand miles down the mighty Indus, of which the Shyok is only a tributary.

It was at the close of a short Tibetan day that Rex Bavington and I were sitting in our home by the light of a hurricane lamp. Suddenly our little "four by two" door was pulled open and Fazl called in anxiously, "Come and hear this strange noise; people are running about, shouting to one another. They seem terrified!" We rushed for the door, ducking our heads in the process, and hurried with Fazl to an open part of the house. We stood quietly listening. Away over at the base of the mighty mountain where the Shyok sweeps round in a deep and swift curve came a continual booming and rumbling. Fear touched us as with icy fingers.

We had prayed together before getting our coats to set off for the river, but were soon halted. Already the waters were seen shimmering among the apricot trees of the village fields. People rushed about as if demented, as the great valley filled with water from mountain to mountain. It looked as if we were doomed. What should we do? Back first of all to the old flat-roofed house for consideration and prayer. We rose from our knees resolved to stay with the people and bear witness to Christ in their tragedy no matter what happened. Fazl and Khaliq slipped out into the night and we followed carrying only a medicine chest, matches (for the people of these regions use only flint and tinder), extra socks, and a Bible.

People seemed to be hurrying everywhere. Old and

young were carrying their rough flour, turnips, carrots, dried apricots, and hens. One old man was rushing about demented, shaking his lighted brand wildly and shouting loudly in front of the oncoming waves of hungry waters. We stripped off our coats. Lantern in hand we entered houses where people worked desperately, and desperately we worked with them. The water was lapping only six feet from the walls of one humble home we entered. In their fear the Baltis lifted superhuman loads. One load which I had been hardly able to move, I saw a young lad lift and carry away on his back. Rex used his topi to bale out the coarse flour into old blankets. The flour spilled on to his wet face when he put it on again. I remember one young Balti woman who was an inspiration, so calm, quiet, and ready to help with anything and everything. She even gave up the valued black cord threaded into her own black plaits. A Balti cut it off and tied up the mouth of a sack. The continual hitting of one's head against the low rafters of a house with the apprehension of knowing that the waters might have cut one off when one came out, was a trying experience.

Outside I looked around. No children were to be seen. Only the old man kept up his running with the lighted brushwood, ever watching and shouting at the oncoming waters. The Balti women no longer ran away at our approach. They lost all shyness and one even caught hold of me pulling me along to help her.

Everyone was terror-stricken and we were far from happy! The full moon rose over the jagged peaks to light up a dismal scene. We entered a little mill and baled out the last of the ground flour into an old blanket.

We looked across our great and broad valley listening to the pounding waters at the base of the mountains. The cold sea stretched away into the distance, and in the eerie shadows of the houses on higher ground furtive figures darted to and fro. We now decided to go and see how our own home had fared. To our joy it was still high and dry. Our concern sent us to look for Fazl and Khaliq, and we found them near a flood mark. We watched the waters play at that tell-tale mark. It seemed to say, "The Lord has said, 'Thus far and no farther'." The waters had spent themselves and were going down. We thanked God for His stepping in to save us. The great sea gleamed and shone in the cold clear air of the Tibetan night, but it no longer menaced us. Tired, wet, and weary we climbed back home for something to eat. Then we reached for the accordion and the Baltis around us sat listening to our praising the Lord.

WA-SE-LEEN

"*My God; in Him will I trust*" Psalm 91: 2.

HESTER WITHEY *China*

THE rickety old truck groaned its way up, up, and around awe-inspiring corners of the mountain road. Terraced rice paddies spread out in their patchwork splendour. But all was not going smoothly. Those flooded rice fields served another purpose. The chugging truck had a radiator that persisted in acting like a sieve rather than a tank. Since every two or three miles there was a convenient rice field from which a leaky basin could scoop muddy water to replenish the supply in the radiator, travel could be resumed again—all in accord with local "service-station" techniques.

A disquieting fact, however, was the incurable persistence of the tyres in going flat, or producing punctures. Considering that they were held together by rubber patches secured in place by metal rivets, nuts and bolts, this was not surprising. The unconventional device worked for surprisingly long periods, but the odds were against its effectiveness indefinitely. On such occasions the driver, with true Chinese equilibrium, would remark to his passengers, "Just now, please be so kind as to enjoy a little leisure and relaxation"; which, being interpreted meant, "Please get out of the car, and make up your minds to sit on the roadside for a few hours, whatever the weather, while we see if we can get these scraps of tyre together again." And, of course, when such interruptions came frequently, these periods of "relaxation" lengthened into nights spent in dingy inns along the road. The hours of darkness were kept alive by the unwearying attendance of armies of bugs that crawled from every crack and crevice of the furniture and walls of the rooms.

How did this peculiar journey begin? The two missionary ladies were travelling inland in West China, aiming for the plateau lands of the Eastern Tibetan area at that time under the Chinese Nationalist Government. The back of the covered truck was piled full of medical equipment, supplies for other missionaries already stationed in this hinterland, and the personal goods of the travelling ambassadors of the Cross. There was a good bus service between these two towns, but the regular buses would not take extra baggage, and so kind Chinese friends had unwittingly given the wrong advice, "Hire a truck from this company, and they will take you and your baggage." Not knowing any better, the suggestion had been accepted. Men missionaries might have thought to look into the condition of the truck, but we were mere women and happily got in without a thought as to whether the contraption would go or not!

The vehicle was roaring and chugging its way laboriously on, around a corner and on to a fairly level spot, when the driver suddenly stopped. He hastily got out of the car, took a look at the front wheel, and turned white. He sank down on the roadside, utter fear and desolation written all over his face. The "grease-monkey", a lad who accompanied the driver to take care of the dirty work, and the two passengers got out also to look. The hub-cap of the front wheel was gone, and the wheel itself, minus an assortment of its bolts and fastenings, was dangling on the end of the front axle-rod. Why it had not completely rolled off on some of those turns of the road no one quite knew. But it hadn't!

With patient resignation, interspersed with superstitious mutterings, the driver managed to muster enough courage to try to fasten the wheel on again. He and his assistant worked and hammered, bent the metal, and finally thought they had the wheel securely knocked into place. So the journey proceeded.

But no, now the wheel was smoking from the friction caused by the absence of that necessary commodity, axle-grease. It had completely disappeared during the violent treatment the wheel had received, and the men had not thought about this detail. But, fortunately, they knew enough not to go on without it. But what could be done? There was no vestige of axle-grease in the car supplies. The wide stretches of paddy fields spread as far as the eye could see—good for the radiator, but not good for axle-grease. The nearest sizeable towns were miles and miles away. No welcoming service-station signs scintillated in the sunshine; no passing vehicle brought aid; no autopatrol or garage to ring up; no phone; no telegraphic office within reach . . . nothing . . . nothing . . . as far as the eye could see, or imagination run. "We could be parked here for days," they mused, "before help could be summoned." In the meanwhile we would have to walk miles to get food, while the load would be exposed to bandits or thieves, of whom the driver might be an associated member! Obviously he had no bright ideas either. Pale and despairing, he sat by the road and insisted that fate was against us. The truck could not go any farther, there was nothing he could do, and he saw no sense in assuming any responsibility in the matter. They could do what they liked, and that was that!

Many times during that trip the missionaries had sent heart "telegrams" to the heavenly Headquarters from which they had received the "Go ye into all the world, and preach the Gospel to every creature". But now they decided to do so publicly—that God might be glorified in whatever deliverance came—for either He delivered, or there was no deliverance. So, together they stood and prayed aloud to the God of heaven, told

Him they trusted Him to intervene and show His great power, told Him they loved Him whatever He chose to do, or not do—and waited.

A short time elapsed, and then along came the "grease-monkey" with a message from the driver, who was sitting a few yards away, "Please, honourable teachers, have you any 'wa-se-leen'?"

"Never heard of it," was their first reaction, but they repeated the word over and over, trying to figure out the big idea; no Chinese word seemed to fit the bill. Then suddenly something registered. "Oh, you mean 'Vaseline'!" Somewhere in the great wide world of China they had heard of the wonders of Western medicine, and the word had stuck. "But, no," they thought, "we do have 20 lb. of Vaseline in our medical supplies, but that is in a banded box at the very back of this truck. How can we get at that without unloading the whole thing?" With only those two feeble men, the women realized it was an almost impossible job. Inwardly they questioned Headquarters, "Is that what You want, Lord?"

Then light dawned! "What is *like* Vaseline?" thought the new missionary nurse. "Oh yes, I know!" and she dashed to her first-aid kit in the handy baggage available for the journey, and pulled out a partly-used tube of a strong-smelling methylated ointment, meant to be used as a liniment, called "Balm Bengue"—the texture was much like Vaseline. This was duly presented to the driver. He and his accomplice unscrewed the cap, and the strong odour hit them immediately.

"Um, very good medicine; yes, very good medicine," they commented. No time was lost in removing the battered wheel, and a generous application of Balm Bengue was smeared where axle grease is supposed to be. The wheel was replaced. Surely some heavenly guardian kept his hand on that wheel and the Balm Bengue! It acted like a charm. All problems with the front wheel were solved. When they said, "No way at all! Impossible! Can't be done" . . . it was then that God stepped in!

IN THE SWATH OF THE SICKLE

"*Under His wings shalt thou trust*" Psalm 91: 4.

MARGARET WILLIAMS *China*

THE morning express pulled out of Kalgan Station and gathered speed for the long descent to the plains of Peiping. We were due in the late afternoon. I had my plans well laid for a quick shopping trip before returning to our northern city on the Great Wall. I tried to settle down for a restful journey and quiet reading.

It was May 1948. There was unrest throughout the whole of North China. The Communists were closing in on strategic centres, and were carrying out a programme of harrassment by cutting railways, destroying bridges, and making surprise attacks on villages. The line on which I was travelling that morning had been cut once or twice some weeks before, but all had been so quiet since then that I dared to risk this quick visit for necessary business and shopping. In view of the political unrest my husband had advised against the trip, but my insistence that all would be well, and that I could quickly make the trip to Peiping and return, finally won, and he had consented to try to get a travel pass for me and to buy my ticket. We were planning to leave the next week for Kalgan for a long trek to the extreme western borders of China, where we hoped to be safe from Communist restrictions and to be able to push evangelistic work in pioneer regions.

But here I was on the morning express, having just said goodbye to him at the station. As the train was starting, he had put his hand in the open window for one last quick grasp. Hours later I wondered if that was his last touch I had received.

The train gained speed and a strange foreboding grew in my heart. Instead of being able to settle down for a restful journey and a few hours of reading, uneasiness possessed me. There were not many women on the train and certainly no other foreign woman, so naturally I attracted attention. A gentleman was sitting opposite me who, I learned afterwards, was an official in the Nationalist Government. Wanting to engage in conversation, he moved over to face me, and politely questioned me with all that might be expected in getting acquainted. My new friend's kindness made a measure of courtesy necessary, so at lunch time I offered him a sandwich from what I had brought with me. When opportunity afforded, I quietly prayed in my heart and sought comfort from the Word. But all seemed dark and no help came, only the increasing heaviness of heart. Had I disobeyed God in coming? Had self once more insisted on its way, although the reasons for making the journey seemed urgent? My testimony of being a Christian and believing in a God who answers prayer, brought polite questions from Mr. Ch'i, my new friend, but in my own ears my words sounded ineffectual. However, I did what I could to make plain the claims of Christ on his life.

Again and again we were held up by passing troop-trains loaded with soldiers. Our fast express was proceeding very slowly. At mid-afternoon the word came that Communists had attacked and cut the line at the Nankou Pass. We would not reach Peiping that night! Concern now turned to fear. Mr. Ch'i talked a lot with one or two railway officials who happened to be in the coach. I found a quiet corner where I poured out my heart to the Lord.

Shortly after, Mr. Ch'i asked me if I would take the risk with a few others to return to Kalgan. Hope leaped up in my heart and I told him I had just been asking God to make this possible. An empty troop-train was coming north, and the officials had given permission for us to get on that train with the hope of being able to leave the danger zone. There were five of us: Mr. Ch'i and his servant, a station-master of a small station just out of Kalgan, and a train conductor who wanted to join his train at one of the stations north of us.

When the northbound train arrived, there was but one car where passengers were allowed, and it was already filled with frightened, silent men and one woman. The coach was really like a luggage van with seats down the sides and two rows down the centre. I found a corner and sought for courage in prayer. We moved slowly through the countryside in the darkness. Suddenly our attention was drawn to a fire over by the mountains. The Communists had fired a village. Tension increased, and I tried to prepare myself for whatever might come. I put on what extra clothing I could, and gathered all of value into one small bag easily carried.

The train stopped. We were at a station, but all was dark and ominously quiet. There was absolute silence in the coach and tension was real. Without warning bursts of firing broke out all around us. It seemed to come from all sides. Passengers fell to the floor and under the seats for safety. Then someone said "Run!" I could not move. My face was buried in my arms as I crouched under the seat, calling on God. Before I knew how it happened, I was alone in the dark coach. I cried to God. "O God, protect; let none of their shells take effect; be our shield; You *are* our shield; put them to flight." I cautiously tried to leave the coach by a centre door, but something stopped me. I felt Someone check me. Back in my corner such fear gripped my heart in my helplessness.

Crouching there, I remembered some years before facing a fuller consecration than I had ever known, taking the identity of the Cross in all it might mean for me. When Jesus seemed most precious, I boldly declared that I would gladly suffer all for Him, and Satan had suddenly suggested that if I followed all the way, that would mean death at the hands of the Communists. He had suggested a form of death, which I had heard the Communists were using on victims, so awful that I had shuddered in fear and dread. For some time I had struggled against these suggestions, then Jesus had assured me He would be in control of all my circumstances, and comfort came. Now, as I huddled there in the dark with the shells of the Communists all around, the thought came: "This is it; that experience you had those years ago saying you would go all the way with Jesus is now coming to pass. Outside this coach is the place of your death." Fear so gripped me that I could scarcely breathe. I cried to God to take fear from me and let me be a true witness for Him, but only chilling fear remained. What should I do? It seemed the attacking Communists might enter the coach at any minute. Should I once more try to run? But where?

Quite suddenly the door at the end of the coach was opened, and my first thought was, "They are here!" By the faint glimmer of moonlight I saw a young soldier and realized that he was as frightened as I was. I can still hear his whisper, "Who are you? Where is your baggage? Follow me quickly." Without waiting for more, he quickly grabbed my two small bags and was gone. I could just glimpse him jump from the train and run across an open space between the train and the wall of the town. As he darted through an opening, I sought to follow as best I could. I stumbled across the open space and into the dark alley. In a corner behind the buildings I found the other passengers hiding. My young soldier helped me to a corner where we all waited in silence. The firing continued, and at each sound we feared our hiding-place was discovered. At length, the young soldier told me to follow him, and in the dark we made our way to a safer place between some stacks of hay. There was space between the hay and a mud wall where seven of us found room to crouch. It was getting on into the night and the cold increased. I burrowed into the hay for warmth. The moon was gone, and it began to rain.

Off and on through the night the firing continued, but at five o'clock in the morning there was a strange calm. The young soldier disappeared, and once more fear gripped me. Again I said to my Father, "You are my shield; You are my shield." The young soldier returned and again bade me follow him. He had my bags safely in his keeping, and led me to a mud house where the family had been keeping vigil through the night. They had a fire and hot water, and the shelter and warmth of the little mud room were a comfort indeed. I was able to wash, get the straw from my clothing and hair, and felt refreshed.

Just then I heard a familiar voice outside the door,

"Mrs. Williams! Are you safe? Are you all right? Oh, what a night! Your God has answered prayer!" It was my official friend, Mr. Ch'i. When the firing had started the night before, he was off the train trying to persuade the station-master to let the train proceed to the north. In the danger of the firing he could not return to the coach but had found safety elsewhere. He said we must leave if at all possible, for the Communists would return the next night. We must get away. He took me to the railway station where we had hot tea to drink, and where I could lie down in a quiet room. I was soon asleep from exhaustion, but before long Mr. Ch'i excitedly awakened me, saying, "There is a chance we can go north. They may start the train and we can go towards Kalgan. We must get on and be ready."

As I followed Mr. Ch'i towards the train, I caught a glimpse of my young soldier friend at some distance. How my heart went out to him with gratitude. I never saw him again. Was he under Communist fire at the Front when brave Chinese boys gave their lives in the losing fight? Was he taken prisoner or forced into the Red Army? Is he living today? Each thought of him brings warmth to my heart. I could only commit him to God's keeping on that May morning.

A strange sense of unreality filled me as once more I found myself in that railway coach where I had been hiding the night before. As I sat in my corner, now bright with sunlight, hoping against hope that the train would start, I looked at the place where the Communists had been firing at the station and the town. Had I alighted from the train as I started to do the night before, I would have stepped right into the midst of the Communists. They were attacking from that side.

I opened my New Testament and this time God spoke clearly. My eyes fell on a little promise card which I had put in for a book-mark, "Fear not; I am thy shield . . ." With a quick gasp of faith and joy I knew God was with me. At long last His presence was real. I hurried to Mr. Ch'i and said, "God has given me a promise. He is our shield. He will save us." Excitedly he told the few others who were with us and who were hoping for escape from that danger spot, that the missionary lady had a promise from her God and we would all be safe! Again and again he told it. At last the train was moving. We were actually leaving that place of danger. We were moving northward. How bright the sunshine! How blue the sky! How lovely the little pink flowers on the mountain-side! The joy of deliverance flooded my heart. God had answered every prayer that my lips had breathed during that dreadful night. The Communist shells had not taken effect. God had been our shield. He had sent them back. For some strange reason they had moved away from the town.

The Communists had not been so kind at a station some miles down the line. A simultaneous attack had been made there. The station and train were burned, and eighty prisoners taken off to the mountains, among them the train conductor who had been with us and who had hoped to join his train. I saw him later and heard his testimony of a miraculous escape. God had even answered my prayers for him!

The next night the Communists returned to burn the station, and attacked the town where we had been protected. But we were safely away.

BLOOD ON THE ORANGE BLOSSOM

"*He that dwelleth in the secret place of the most High shall abide under the shadow of the Almighty*" Psalm 91: 1.

PEGGY EASTON *Colombia*

As a missionary in Colombia, South America, I never imagined that ahead of me lay an experience which would cause me to reach what is commonly known as "rock bottom". I was to prove in a very real way the presence and provision of God. It seemed difficult to think that my faith and peace of mind could be so rudely challenged, but it happened on a beautiful tropical evening in Mariquita in the year 1951. It was a night like so many others of happy memory spent in that lovely little town. My husband and I were holding a weekly class for young people. The air was still warm with the heat of a hot day. The hens over the fence in our neighbour's garden clucked and shuffled as they settled down on their perches for the night. The night insects sang their chorus; the bats wove their lightning courses in and out of the shadows. In the church, the moths danced their giddy whirls around the electric light bulbs, eventually to fall, quivering and broken, on to the red concrete floor. They looked like so many victims of an air disaster. The atmosphere was heavy, laden with the perfume of tropical flowers, gardenias, roses, orange blossom, and many others, and high in the sky a full moon looked down from cold isolation seemingly conscious of a beauty all her own.

Soon, a few young people gathered for the class, and we all sat down on our hard wooden benches. We were glad for yet another opportunity to worship God and for freedom to study His precious Word. I say, "yet another opportunity" with reason. Many groups such as ours had been forbidden to congregate, and their churches had been confiscated or destroyed in these times of trouble and bloodshed. In the middle of our service we were suddenly attacked by a group of the local police. Chaos reigned within the little hall as blows were dealt right and left on the defenceless men. My husband received wounds which afterwards necessitated stitches by one of the town's doctors. It all happened so quickly! In no time, it seemed, they were being marched off, veritable spectacles with their clothing dirty, torn, and bloodstained. They were taken to the police-barracks to be at the mercy of a few evil men, victims of cruel and devilish punishments for four long hours.

With their gaolers behind them armed to the teeth, they disappeared around the corner of the village square. I then locked the church door and its outer gate. As I walked slowly up the grassy road with Lawrence, our little son of nearly six years of age, I was met by the wife of one of the young men. She panted as she ran towards us. Rosario, a young girl who had been in the service, had run like the wind to tell her that we had been attacked. "Oh, Señora Peggy! What shall we do!" "First of all, I am coming to your house for prayer," I said, "and then I must get home. If the men should be released, I must be there when they come." We continued talking in whispers as we hurried to her small cottage at the roadside. Closing the doors firmly, we sank to our knees at the side of the kitchen table at which she had been busy ironing. Pressed garments were hanging all around the room. There was scarcely time to think, it seemed. Yet, as a result of having read and meditated upon the Word of God certain principles have been worked into our hearts. These manifest themselves in times of need and spiritual emergency. "If I regard iniquity in my heart, the Lord will not hear me." I was not conscious of that verse, but as soon as I opened my mouth to pray these words rushed out, "If any of us have sinned in any way, let us now confess it." The issues were tremendous—perhaps even the lives of four servants of the Lord. We asked God to cleanse us, and then into His hands we commended our loved ones. He alone was all-powerful, all-knowing, and His presence was everywhere. There was little we could say. Our hearts were too full, too heavy. Prayer was but a cry for help.

As we rose from our knees the señora said, "You must not be seen on the road. You must get away through the fence at the back of the house." So we crept out quietly, Lawrence, Rosario, and I. The street was completely empty of people. Although it was not yet nine o'clock, every citizen was behind closed doors, afraid to be abroad. Bad news travels fast. They knew that the enemy was at large in search of victims. As we slipped along, passing two or three houses silent and white beneath the brilliant light of the moon, I felt as if I were walking in a dream! It was all so unreal, so impossible! My husband and the others whisked away under the threat of knives and revolvers, to what . . . ? So utterly alone we seemed as we moved along, the dry grass hard and slippery beneath our feet. Eventually, in this silent world, we reached our house. I unlocked the door and entered. How empty it looked and felt. Lawrence and Rosario, spent with crying, were put to bed and soon sleep claimed them. The house was quiet except for the squeaking of the bats as they shot in through the eaves, and the "zoom" of a mosquito persistently attacking.

And now, like Jacob, I was left alone. What thoughts of turmoil and confusion pressed into my mind! Was it really true? Had this thing happened, and to us? Reason said, "Oh, the injustice of it all! Innocent men taken away as criminals, attacked by those who knew them to be unarmed, and, as Christians, unlikely to defend themselves. How unfair!" Faith in God said, "Lord, protect them! Rout their enemies! Give Thy servants words which will confound their persecutors! Preserve them from danger and spare their lives!" And so it went on, as I knelt by the side of the bed. A battle raged in my heart and mind. No peace, no light! All darkness. Praying in the darkness! The truth was, I did not know *how* to pray. Satan said, "For all you know, they may now be dead! Perhaps they have been taken away to another area, and, as you know well, some never come back again." All this I knew without being told. The country was in its third year of civil and political strife and bloodshed.

The hours were dragging on. Nine-thirty; ten o'clock, and then eleven. Still I struggled, reminding myself of so many precious promises, clinging to them as, if drowning, I would to a lifebelt. And then, in His own incomparable love and compassion God came and spoke to me in the stillness of the room. He asked a simple question, "In whose hands are they? In those of their persecutors, or in Mine?" "In Thy hands," I replied. "Since they are in My hands, then I am responsible for them. I am in charge. Whatever happens, good or seeming ill, I am there with them. Unless I give permission, no man can touch them. I have chosen them for this hour, and My will is good." The blessed will of God! No need to struggle any longer. The Lord continued, "Whatever happens, *My will is best*, even should I allow them to be taken to the farthest limit—to death." Immediately, a light illumined my mind, and a great peace flooded my soul. They were in God's hands, and He gently led me to the point where I could say to Him, "Yes, Lord, whatever happens . . . I am at peace."

The room was quiet. Only the gentle breathing of the two sleepers broke its stillness. It was now later than half-past eleven, and I was so tired and exhausted. The emotional strain and spiritual struggle of the past hours had drained all strength away. There was no need to pray any longer, nor could I. Shortly afterwards I retired, feeling, nevertheless, ashamed that I could do so when my dear husband and the others were—who knew where? But the Lord knew, and because He knew and had come to my aid, I now could rest. Later I understood as never before something of the truth of Romans 8: 26, 27, "Likewise the Spirit helpeth our infirmities: for we know not what we should pray for as we ought: but the Spirit Himself maketh intercession for us with groanings which cannot be uttered. And He that searcheth the hearts knoweth what is the mind of the Spirit, because He maketh intercession for the saints according to the will of God." How very wonderful! When we do not know *how* to pray, He knows and prays for us.

Next morning at five o'clock a knock came at the door. It was the Señora Rosana, mother of Saul, who, as I later learned, bore himself so valiantly for Christ during the ordeal of that night. We spoke of what had taken place, and then arranged to go along to the prison with food. Beds, too, might be needed later if they should be detained for any length of time. "Of course," said Rosana, "they may not be there now. Sometimes they take such prisoners away and kill them!" "Yes," I answered, "I know that is true. But I believe God has spared them." "Amen!" was her fervent reply. What a grand soldier of Christ she had always been! No complaints!

We set out for the prison and were allowed to converse for a few minutes with the four who had been through the fiery furnace for their Master, and with Him, too! My husband said, "About a quarter to twelve we were released from the hands of our tormentors and escorted here. The head of the prison is a good man and friendly towards us. He has already attended to my wounds." A quarter to twelve! That was the hour when, worn out, I had unwillingly gone to bed! Now I saw that indeed there had been no need for further prayer. God had stepped in! All glory be to Him!

THE VIRGIN OF THE SALT MINE

"*I will deliver him*" Psalm 91: 15.

PAT SYMES *Colombia*

It was a special feast day in the large country town of Zipaquira. Crowds of gaily-dressed people were happily jostling one another in the narrow streets, townspeople in all their Sunday glory, men and maidens full of life, shouting and laughing to one another as they passed from street to street. Crowds of country people, the women with long, wide, many-coloured pleated skirts and the men with different-coloured homespun cloaks and black hats, congregated in little groups in the central square, laughing, talking and joking. The sun was shining brilliantly from a deep blue cloudless sky on this beautiful afternoon in January of 1936. The air was warm and crisp on the extensive fertile table land 8,000 feet above sea level, four degrees north of the Equator. A chain of broken hills and mountains, shooting up to 10,000 feet, encircle this plateau. Away to the south a snowy peak rarely seen stayed hidden in a haze of distant clouds.

The old cathedral tower overshadows the square, towering high above all the other buildings, grey, domineering, and silent, ominous in its strength and silence. The tower clock struck 2.30 p.m. The great cedar doors of the cathedral were opened wide on this special day. The multitude of country folk looked up in awe and wonder at the church in which they placed all their hope for eternal life. Conversation ceased as they gazed into the solemn depths of the sanctuary. They could just discern the flower-decked altar, illuminated by myriads of candles. They paused; women crossed themselves and murmured, "Ave Maria", while men bent the knee and passed onward. They had been in the holy sanctuary that very morning. It had been crowded with people, so full that hundreds had to remain outside on the spacious pavement. They had seen the priest in his holy vestments while the choir had sung sweetly high away in the choir loft. They had joined with the crowd in responses. They had seen the host lifted up and had fallen on their knees as the words of their priest changed the wafer into the body and blood of Jesus. They believed the Son of God had come down from heaven as the cloud of incense rolled across upward. Jesus was in His temple and they had all knelt silently upon the cold stone floor. The incense had partly obscured the Mother of God who stood high and stately against the high altar, holding the child Jesus on one arm and the rosary on the other. They had seen the lovely face of their Mother. She would intercede with her Son because He would not deny her anything. He would then perhaps make petition to God austere and stern and so far away from them.

They had now fulfilled their obligations. They had paid vows to their favourite saint, and to the Virgin. A mother is very lenient and allows her children to have a bit of fun, especially today, so fun they were having. Gambling tables edged the square, where people could gain from ten to twenty times the amount staked. Perhaps the Virgin or a saint would give you luck if they were promised a good part of the gains. At the foot of the church steps were stalls where thirst could be slaked. The priest had pretty girls there selling beer, rum, and even "fire water", and all gains were for the church and for the "father". This was a great day!

It would soon be nightfall. The majority would need to be helped along the homeward track. Coarse laughter and unholy jesting would be heard as the lengthening shadows drew across the holy day. Men would fight over an insult—half-drunken wives and daughters would jostle one another and try to keep the peace. Hard words would follow a shouted dirty conversation. In a heated argument, one hit another on the head. The offender was kicked in the stomach. A knife flashed in the dim moonlight, and amid groans and shrieks he fell with a gaping cut from eye to ear. The other swooned, oozing blood from a deep red wound in the body. Life ebbed away. Wives wailed, daughters wept, sons swore vengeance, and the rest disappeared silently into the night. Death! And what after that? They had died too quickly for their last confession, and for the "father" to bring the host. There was no opportunity for absolution of their sins.

The Virgin of the Salt Mine had been exalted in the great meeting at 11 a.m. Young girls clothed in pure white had sung her praises. Crowds of worshippers had crushed by with lighted candles to place before her. The throng had gone on leaving the Virgin all alone amid the glare and smoke of many dying candles. The crowd went out into the blaze of the sunshine, out to the beer shops or down the street to the railway station. It was now just about three o'clock in the afternoon and shortly the trains from Chiquinquira and Bogota would arrive at the junction. This great open station-square was the usual place where sweethearts met. Friends also gathered talking in groups; idlers passed away a few more minutes.

Suddenly interest quickened and the crowd gathered at one point. A man and a few women were singing, and they were not merry with drink. Get a bit closer to hear! What is this about Jesus dying on the Cross, shedding His blood, being buried, and rising again, that He lives today—and is coming back again? Well, some of this is new. The tall fair fellow spoke the language fairly well in spite of being a foreigner. Listen! "There is only one Mediator between God and man." "Jesus is the only Mediator because He bore in His own body the sins of the whole world." Father M—— never spoke like that. There he was listening! Some asked him what it was all about. He answered, "These people are the Protestant devils who have been living in this town for two years now. This liberal government that we have, God curse it, gives these heretics liberty and protection. Liberty of religion! There is only one religion, the Holy Roman Catholic Church! The day will come when we will make this government fall, then just wait and see what we will do with this vermin! They are only fit for fire, and fire they will have. Don't listen to them! They don't believe in God or the Virgin."

The man finished and there fell over the crowd an evil hush. Then a murmur rose to a shout, "Kill the Protestant dogs! Don't defile our town with your teaching!" The crowd fell back. Father M—— had gone! At a word from the man the three women stole away. One of the ladies stood watching in suspense. She was the wife of the preacher. Another hurried off to find the police. (They should have been there to keep order, but were locked in the barracks in case they got drunk, for they would need to be sober later in the day!) Two strong men closed in on the tall preacher. They meant dirty work! One of them had a great steel spanner more than a foot long and the other a piece of iron, both lethal weapons. Suddenly one man let out a kick and the preacher doubled up, but he was not down.

Badly hurt, he did not run, but edged himself away, protecting himself with his arms. He backed away to avoid a cruel stab. "In the name of the Virgin, kill the Protestant dog!" His back was now against the station wall. He did not seem to have the look of a devil. He could at least fight, but he did not attempt to. Cowards do not openly preach and risk their lives for a belief. Look! The two now attacked him—that kick missed—he was too quick! Why didn't they use that iron bar? What was wrong with them? They could have hit him a dozen times by now! The iron bars were raised to hit him again when their arms fell to their sides. They could not hit him. Was there some unseen power protecting the fellow?

The young woman who hovered on the fringe of the crowd was surrounded by a group of students who had just come up. "Don't be afraid, miss!" they called. "We will protect you." "I don't need protection!" she answered. "Help him over there! They are going to kill him! Oh, go quickly! They will kill him!" The students immediately surrounded the preacher. One grabbed the hand of the would-be killer who had the bar high again. The boys escorted the preacher to safety. God had stepped in. He did so again and again through the terrible yet wonderful years of persecution in Colombia.

An unforgettable climax to an unforgettable time; the preacher and his wife had been married only yesterday.

MIDDAY MADNESS

"*Thou shalt not be afraid for . . . the destruction that wasteth at noonday*" Psalm 91: 5, 6.

GERTRUDE HOLLOWAY *Liberia*

WEDDING bells had rung for Percy and Iva Clubine and for Cyril and myself at a double ceremony in Tappi Ta. All four Gio pioneers felt their joy and happiness knew no bounds as Percy and Iva remained at this station and as Cyril and I prepared to leave for the Gio station at Garplay.

As there is no motor road between Tappi Ta and Garplay, it necessitates a journey of eighty miles (on foot) through high African bush. This journey was to be our honeymoon! Just as we were ready to depart our host called to me, "Look around the corner of the house; your Honeymoon Express awaits you!" What I saw was four big brawny African men with a hammock frame placed on their heads and a native-made string hammock suspended securely from it. Two men were placed at the front of the hammock and two at the back. This is a common means of transport in the interior. After three and a half days of travel, we arrived at Garplay on Saturday evening after dark.

The next few weeks were happy and full, entering into pioneer missionary work. The treks took us to some of the 120 Gio villages in our area of 60,000 souls; this was the gigantic and yet joyous privilege to shoulder until reinforcements came along.

One Saturday evening a month later, a runner brought a letter from Mr. Staniford, the leader of the W.E.C. in West Africa, informing us that he was to visit the station and the overall work in Liberia. Cyril hurried off quickly to meet him as he would now be nearing the station. The letter telling of his coming had been long delayed!

We had very happy and precious fellowship during the next six days before "Sta" and Cyril departed for Flumpa of the Mano tribe. They were rather reluctant to leave me alone on the station so soon after our marriage. I assured them that it would not be "crusading" to hinder them in any way visiting other stations in different tribes. With this assurance from me, the two men set off through the bush on foot to cover the fifty miles to Flumpa.

The following week I found very busy attending the sick in the increasingly large dispensaries, holding services, and supervising the station work. But Friday, May 26th, could have been a day of tragedy on the Liberian field!

It was midday. The intense heat halted all work. Everyone was resting indoors before resuming the afternoon's work. No one was moving. The workmen had all been sent to the village of Garplay for their noon meal and short rest. All was quiet, when, suddenly, I heard a terrific commotion and the excited voices of men on the front verandah. Running quickly to the door, I opened it. The mission workmen were struggling with a mentally-deranged man who was brandishing high in the air a thick heavy club, shouting, "Let me go! Let me go! I want to kill Missie! I want to kill Missie!" Perspiration was streaming down the bodies of the workmen as they struggled with the poor insane soul. Soon all three were lost to view in the thick bush. Twenty minutes later, the two workmen returned, panting from the struggle. "Oh, Missie," they said, "God blessed you plenty today!" I particularly enquired as to why they were on the Mission at the time instead of being in town, fifteen minutes' walk away. They replied, "God has kept us here for the purpose of saving your life." They had had a "palaver" to talk out and so had retired to a secluded spot on the Mission. When they had finished their affair, they were just on their way to town. Rounding the corner of the missionaries' house, they caught sight of this mentally-afflicted man, with a club in one hand and the other hand on the door ready to enter the room in which I was alone. They sensed something was wrong and shouted an enquiry. The man replied that he was going inside to kill "Missie". Both men pounced upon him immediately, and after a grim struggle forced the demented man to a farm and placed him in the hands of those responsible for him, since there are no mental institutions here. They questioned him as to why he wanted to murder me. He replied that he wanted the young native girl who was in my charge and knew that as long as she was under our care there would be no hope for him! With "Missie" out of the way and Mr. Holloway absent, there would be no hindrance to him! He had not realized that God is the One who is ever watching to deliver from "the destruction at noonday".

BRUISES AND BLESSINGS

"He shall give His angels charge over thee"
Psalm 91: 11.

ALBERT MOORE *Congo*

IT was already getting late, really too late to set out on such a journey, but it was Saturday and if we did not get off it would mean waiting until Monday. All was packed up for a month's trek in the bush, and the Africans who were going with us had also been ready since early morning with their bundles and baskets and babies. Without any hindrance on the road we could make it by dusk, so I decided to start.

The students in the Bible school at Ibambi follow a course of eight weeks' study and then have a month out in different districts evangelizing and witnessing in order that they may be fully experienced for their work. The surrounding areas had been continually visited by these trekkers, and it was felt that others farther afield should now benefit, and people could be taken in the Chevrolet truck to a more distant station. Making this the starting point we would scatter widely among the villages, and come in again at the end of the month. The more we considered this the more it was felt that the Lord would have us go, and yet also there was opposition; not so much outwardly but a consciousness that the enemy was withstanding this effort. With much prayer one difficulty after another was faced and overcome, and then when plans were all made, an unexpected trip took the truck away down south to Lubutu, and it returned late only the night before we hoped to start. The truck also had developed some trouble which had to be attended to. There was no time for an overhaul, but a full morning was spent making it roadworthy. This done, it still had to be loaded.

We were going down to Bomili among the Babari tribe some ninety miles away, where the missionaries were building a new station. They needed a brick machine, so this heavy equipment had to be lashed on board. There were also boxes of stores and some camp equipment. In the remaining space twenty-eight Congolese, students and their wives plus a few babies, had to find a place to sit or stand. All their bundles and sleeping mats were tied to the side or poked in somewhere. Fortunately they easily accommodate themselves, not being used to much comfort, and can happily perch in precarious positions. A large tarpaulin was fastened right over the truck as protection from the weather. There was plenty of happy chatter as they all climbed in and the tailboard at the back was closed. My wife and I with our little girl of twenty months climbed into the cab. The journey started.

Leaving the Ibambi area the road ran on through the gold mines. This has always been considered a very second class road, being kept open only for contact with the mines. Many of these had now ceased to function, so the road was in very bad repair. Holes and ruts made the driver alert to which part of the track to take. The truck moved from side to side and the living load in the back swayed with it. Rain began to fall, not heavy rain, but a drizzle that grew worse as we approached the mountain at Baberu. We looked forward to the distant views from the sides of this mountain, as in the forest we are unable to see beyond the clearing of the mission station. There was disappointment as the misty rain closed in upon us. Only a slow speed could take the mountain road safely and this jeopardised our chance of reaching our destination in daylight. However, we were all in good spirits and were greatly looking forward to the month's evangelism among the Babari tribe. The Congolese were having a good sing in the back of the truck.

Up and round we went, with the rocky mountainside almost perpendicular above us, and sheering off in places with deep drops a few feet from the track. I hoped that we would not have to pass another vehicle! From the passenger seat it was possible to look right into the drop below, so there was a continual prayer-meeting going on next to me. We reached the highest point and then slowly began the descent, twisting and turning, with the drop now on my side. The road was very narrow in places and it was necessary to hug the mountain-side, keeping to the rutted tracks of other vehicles. There was not very far to go when I took a bend in too wide a sweep. The back wheel ran too near the edge of the road. The truck lurched suddenly backwards. I did all in my power to pull back on to the road but the passengers in the back fell in the direction that it slipped. The soft earth gave way and the truck shuddered over the edge. As the vehicle somersaulted our heads hit the roof of the cab and our legs were in the air. My arm was tightly round my little girl and instinctively I called on the Lord to help, not knowing how many times we might somersault before the crash. Over went the truck again and then miraculously it stopped on its wheels about fifty feet below the road. A tree stump had broken the fall and the truck had landed up to its axles in grass and mud not far from a stream.

As I recovered from the shock of the somersault the words came to me, "He shall give His angels charge over thee, to keep thee in all thy ways." "Whose blood is that?" I asked, as something poured down the windscreen. "That's not blood; it's oil." "How many people are killed?" "Let's get out and see." I tried the door, but it was jammed. Men jumped off the back and ran to us, as concerned for us as we were for them. Eventually the cab door was opened and I got out to see if everyone was alive—I had a vision of at least some dead bodies. How could everyone survive with a brick machine, stores, camp equipment, and all those people hurtling head over heels? "It's all right, we are all safe, Mungo iko! (God is!)." The only one badly cut was the man who had jumped out! Beyond bruises, scratches and shock the rest of us were fit. The tarpaulin over the roof had kept our friends from falling out.

It had all happened so quickly, and now we were in real trouble. The night was closing in and the truck was down the mountain-side. How could it be pulled up on to the road again? Suppose it were damaged? Because of the rain we had no idea how far away was the nearest help, so most of the folk scrambled up on to the road while I went to see if I could find help anywhere. Farther along the road I found a mining centre with one or two Belgians in charge. When they heard of our plight they came out in a small car to see what could be done. As they looked over the drop to where my wife was sitting in the cab of the truck, they were amazed and said that it could only be God who had saved us from being killed, and when they saw the cargo and the people that we had on board they felt it impossible to believe that none had been hurt. It was a miracle.

These men were kindness itself. They took us to their camp and gave us an office for a room and arranged transport to take us on to Bomili. A truck was leaving shortly and it would take the whole of our party. They promised to send to their head centre and get block and tackle to haul ours up on to the road. As it would take a day or two to get the tackle they suggested that we all went on to our destination in the mines' car and that I should return later to fetch ours. The men were as good as their word. They winched the truck back on to the road—a remarkable feat, and would not charge us a penny for their work. It was soon running again, though the body was damaged. The month among the Babaris was a great success; the students, recovering from their bruises and scratches, added the story of our deliverance to their testimony in the villages and came back rejoicing telling of souls saved in many places.

BATTLE OF BRITAIN

"*Because he hath set his love upon me therefore will I deliver him*" Psalm 91: 14.

JESSIE SCHOLES *Congo*

IN 1939 war broke out when we were on furlough from Congo. The prospect for missionaries anxious to return to their sphere of service overseas was very black indeed. The Battle of the Atlantic was raging, and boats carrying passengers were few and far between. The difficulties of obtaining berths seemed insurmountable.

We were a party of six and were booked to sail in October 1940. For security reasons the names of boats and ports of embarkation were not disclosed. Passengers were notified to be ready to sail at short notice. Our farewell meetings had been held, trunks and suitcases packed. Each day the odd bit of washing was done for our four-year-old child so that there would not be too much of a rush at the last minute when the expected letter arrived. Instead came a telegram from the Mission Headquarters informing us that the sailing had been cancelled. This was a tremendous disappointment, but we knew that God had allowed it. Now was an opportunity to prove that "All things are possible to him that believeth." Truly war had risen against us but in this we were confident that our God would step in and deliver us.

Many Christian friends were praying, but the answer was delayed. Christmas came and still no news. We enquired about the possibility of flying to Lisbon and sailing from there to Matadi. It was possible, but with a waiting list of hundreds, it would probably be months before we could leave these shores that way. Word from Headquarters said that they were leaving no stone unturned to obtain passages for us. We longed to get back to Congo for we knew there was plenty of work waiting for us.

News then came that it might be possible for the men to go alone. Women and children were not encouraged to travel because of war hazards. We were quite prepared to separate if it were necessary, but felt that the Lord's will was for us all to travel together. The next morning God spoke through His Word in Exodus 10: 11, 26. Pharaoh had said to Moses, "Go now ye that are men, and serve the Lord", but Moses had replied that they would all go and their cattle; "There shall not an hoof be left behind." Then God spoke to Moses and said, "When he shall let you go, he shall surely thrust you out hence altogether" (Exodus 11: 1). These words came as a confirmation to our faith that God would open up the way for us.

We heard of missionaries in like circumstances who were settling down to service in the homeland, but we had no liberty to do this. God had promised, and He would step in at the right time and deliver us. One morning early in May a letter came from one of the party. They had been asked to take over the representation of the Mission in Northern Ireland seeing as there was no prospect of their returning to Congo during the War. We knew that this was not God's will and we felt desperate. Suddenly, shortly after reading the letter, it was as though God spoke, Why don't you write certain shipping agents and enquire from them about the possibility of obtaining passages? They were not our usual agents, but God had spoken, so immediately a letter was typed and sent. Within two days the reply came, "The sailings to Matadi have been little interfered with, and there is a sailing in about three weeks' time; we have contacted your Headquarters and they have told us to go ahead with the bookings." Truly God had stepped in, and we felt as if we were suddenly emerging from captivity into freedom.

A letter was sent off to the others to tell them of the good news. "Hope deferred maketh the heart sick: but when the desire cometh, it is a tree of life." We were soon to meet in Liverpool and embark together. Meanwhile, Liverpool was under heavy bombardment. Night after night the city was a target for the enemy planes, and considerable damage was done. The Battle of

Britain was raging. Would we ever be able to leave these shores? We held on in prayer and faith. Yet when God opens a door no man can shut it. He then opened the way for us and within three weeks of writing to the agent we embarked at Liverpool. I shall never forget passing through that bomb-scarred city. Many enemy planes had been over the previous night leaving a trail of desolation and sorrow behind. The boat on which we sailed was the *Copacabana* of the Belgian line. She had sailed out of Antwerp as the port fell into enemy hands, and since then had been plying between Liverpool and Matadi.

It seemed as though God's protecting care was overshadowing that boat for it proved to be a lifeline to the Congo field during the War. There were 150 Free French troops on board, besides a few other passengers. A small group of missionaries met us in one of the passage-ways as we were going to and from our cabins settling in for the journey. One said, "What is going to happen to us on this voyage? Are you afraid?" "Afraid? Oh no," was the reply. "The Lord has given us the promise of a safe passage. 'He led them on safely, so that they feared not: but the sea overwhelmed their enemies' (Psalm 78: 53)." It was God's word for us all, and they seemed encouraged. We had good fellowship with them through the voyage.

We noticed that the text implied there would be enemies, but God prepared us and gave us that peace and assurance that all would be well. We were only one day in a convoy. As we sailed down the Mersey we saw the funnels of sunken boats protruding above the surface of the water. The same thing could happen to us, but the everlasting arms were around us, protecting us. We were soon out at sea, sailing due west and taking a zig-zag course in order to make it more difficult for any submarine which might be in the vicinity to sight us as a target. A strict look-out was kept night and day by the soldiers who were on board. The ship was blacked out after dusk, and no light of any description was allowed on deck; it was all very weird, but necessary. We soon learned that nature cannot be blacked out. There was a wonderful phosphorescent glow after dark all around the boat at sea level, not usually seen under normal circumstances—another touch of the marvels of God's creation.

This was just after the sinking of the *Bismarck* and the Battle of the Atlantic was at its height. Orders were given that we must be ready to take to the boats at any time, and boat drill took place daily. We were also ordered to have a small package ready with our passports and a few necessities. Most of the passengers slept in their clothes, but we undressed as usual, for had not God promised that He would lead us on safely? We could not doubt His word. Early one morning I was on deck with Daniel, our little boy, and saw a plane in the distance. Others had spotted it and all were ordered below deck immediately. It was an unidentified plane and was flying towards us. The alarm bells sounded and we all made our way to emergency stations. Many of the passengers were still sleeping and had to make a quick exit. It proved to be a false alarm for it was not an enemy plane after all! However, it was good practice.

After a couple of weeks we drew near to Freetown. Two passenger boats had been sunk that week, so extra watch was kept by the soldiers. Suddenly our boat swerved sharply. We did not understand what was happening at the time, but were told later that a torpedo had been fired at us and only the quick action of the helmsman had saved us from the same fate as others. "He led them on safely . . ."

On arriving at Freetown we found the harbour full of shipping and the town full of refugees. We were asked to take some of these on board. They had lost everything except the clothes they stood in. We were there five days during which time a destroyer went out in search of the submarine.

While we were in harbour a plane appeared as if from nowhere. We sat on deck admiring it as it shone in the sun when suddenly the anti-aircraft guns ashore blazed away at it. The aircraft managed to get away, probably back to Dakar, which was then in enemy hands. It was on reconnaissance and had had plenty of time to note the amount and variety of shipping in that large harbour. The bombers were now expected in the night, but God had His own way of dealing with the situation. A tropical storm swept over the town and harbour all night until daybreak. That day we set out to sea and continued our voyage, out of the horrors of war and to arrive in the safety He promised.

MOSQUITOES ARE MESSENGERS

"*My God; in Him will I trust*" Psalm 91: 2.

JIM GRAINGER *Congo*

As tension eased in the political crisis of the Congo and the weeks passed, it was natural for missionaries sheltering in neighbouring Uganda to think of their return. Letters had not come from them until one day three arrived together. Mrs. Grainger wrote telling of the journey across the border and of the stay at the Lea-Wilson Tea Plantation, also of the arrangements by some to proceed to England. She suggested that I would need to come to Uganda with help to drive back the cars of those returning. A plane flight from Paulis was considered, but it was found unlikely and uncertain. A road trip was inevitable. This meant that two men from the Mission station of Ibambi would have to go to Uganda as drivers. But how could two be spared? This problem resolved itself as Arthur Scott arrived in Ibambi from the leprosarium at Malingwia. He was anxious to report to me and to know what had transpired as rumours were confused and conflicting. He would joyfully have gone as an auxiliary driver, but had already driven several hundred miles. He remained at Ibambi and so permitted Frank Cripps, Bill McChesney, and myself to travel.

A four o'clock in the morning departure enabled the three of us to get over the border and into Uganda by evening, and by sharing the driving this was not too strenuous for us. Everything needed for the road was on board the pick-up. There were no incidents on the road and the car behaved magnificently so that excellent time was made. Being well into Uganda, we looked out for a Rest House but none seemed to be located on that road. We decided to stop near a small stream, but not far ahead a side road proved ideal for parking. It certainly was a quiet spot for an undisturbed rest until the morning. Camp beds were put down in the open and a meal prepared. The three of us then went to get some sleep.

Frank Cripps has a deaf ear which he can use to advantage! Once on the bed he kept that ear uppermost and was off into the realms of bliss! I could not sleep and lay listening to the mosquitoes. The night invaders buzzed and whined over us in their attacks, and sleep was impossible. Bill with his twenty-four years of youth was soon asleep. I attempted to rig up my mosquito net, and although this was a noisy operation Frank slept on. I was startled when a voice called out, "Who switched on the light?" It was the full moon which had risen and everywhere was flooded with its light!

Still the mosquitoes attacked. I could not sleep. In the moonlight Bill woke up and we engaged in low conversation. Finally, Frank was awake and generously offered to move off if that seemed advisable. Perhaps it was the best plan, so beds were repacked and the pick-up loaded, and we made a start. Mosquitoes! One of the trio thought they were akin to the messengers of Satan, but he kept hold of the wheel and drove on.

The tarmac road was superb. Not a jolt was felt, and for mile after mile the car skimmed along. Near Fort Portal we ran into a heavy ground mist and the headlights glared back from it creating a white wall in front. The only way to continue was to straddle the central white line. Speed was reduced to a walking pace, and in Fort Portal we had to halt. We did not have a clue as to our right direction. Out of the mist a car suddenly emerged and turned to the right just a few yards ahead of us. We followed. As the lights swept round and across the signpost we read, "Kampala". Travelling now was easier keeping up to the small red rear light of the car ahead. The driver was evidently a local citizen. Later the car stopped and we passed and went on.

The mist thinned and cleared completely. "Keep Left" signs now appeared with regularity. Corners and bends were numerous as the road was twisting continually. The sky lightened as the first signs of daybreak appeared, and the sunrise streaked colours across the sky. I took over the driving.

When daylight was full, we wondered how we were going to contact the returning missionaries. Should we go to Kampala or to the Tea Plantation? Mrs. Grainger had written saying that the road to the Estate was fifty miles west of the city and on the road we were travelling. A look-out was kept for this signboard. In a small town huge signs were directing to many plantations, but the name of Lea-Wilson was not on any of them. We felt we had gone too far and had passed the turning. I stopped and called to a young Baganda going to his office nearby. Could he direct us? "Oh, yes, certainly." He explained that the turning was ten miles back where we had seen all the large boards. In this we proved that the *stops* of a man are ordered of the Lord.

What was happening all this time at the Tea Plantation? They had no knowledge that we were on the way to meet them and so they were planning to return. But God was in control. Their return to Congo had to be made if Government restrictions were to be complied with. The route was planned to be through Kampala, Gole, and Arua and into Congo at Aru. To shorten the trip and to avoid Kampala, which incidentally was out of the way, Mr. Lea-Wilson offered a man to show the convoy a short cut on the Gole road. Eric Smith drove the convoy out at the same time the pick-up was being re-routed.

The guide failed to take the road suggested, but took another that would get the cars on to the Gole route. Down the hill came the leading truck and turned off to the left on to the road chosen by the guide. All the cars were close to ensure all would be together and not miss this turning. Eric stopped the convoy about 100 yards round the corner. At that moment I also turned the corner and drove to pull up behind the convoy. It was timed to a second! A fully complete Mission convoy had naturally lined up! What a reunion! What a time of praise! It could not be asked, "How did it all work out?" for the whole arrangement was absolutely and obviously God's stepping into our plans.

A CHILD'S CALL FOR COURAGE

"*The terror by night*" Psalm 91: 5.

JOY TAYLOR *Congo*

CONGO was emerging independent with birth-pangs of suffering, a suffering that touched the whole world with its gravity and bloodshed. Not far from its epicentre is Lubutu, a distant station of our Congo field. It was 15th February 1961, and the situation in this area had deteriorated rapidly. Reports were reaching us as various "whites" were imprisoned, beaten and maltreated. Truck-loads of soldiers passed by our station and we called our boys, Murray and Barry, and warned them to keep well away from the road, for like all children, they must see every car that passes. At T—— the Roman Catholic priests and sisters were imprisoned. Surely our time had come. We desperately needed a word from the Lord, and on our knees we received it with such directness that our hearts were immediately calmed. It was Psalm 93: 3, 4, "The floods have lifted up, O Lord, the floods have lifted up their voice; the floods lift up their waves. The Lord on high is mightier than the noise of many waters, yea, than the mighty waves of the sea." Then came that assuring injunction in Jeremiah 5: 22, "Fear ye not me? saith the Lord: will ye not tremble at My presence, which have placed the sand for the bound of the sea by a perpetual decree, that it cannot pass it: and though the waves thereof toss themselves, yet can they not prevail; though they roar, yet can they not pass over it?" We felt the Lord had set a bound to the restless waves of violence that so far they might come, but no farther.

Children are very susceptible to situations no matter how we seek to shield and save them from the facts. At bedtime devotions we especially prayed for protection. After the "Amen", Barry looked up and said, "Mummy, how can we get courage?" So we all prayed again specifically for courage no matter what lay ahead. Then in no time they were asleep. Being Friday night our African fellow-workers gathered for fellowship. We discussed the situation and they committed us to the Lord before shaking hands all round to leave. Cyril and I were on our own. We had only one concern and that was for the children. There and then we prayerfully brought them to the Lord, asking that He would deliver them from all fear so that they also would be a testimony. Next morning the children awoke singing. I could not stop them even at the breakfast table! When we lifted Colleen into her high chair, she joined in with three spontaneous "Hallelujahs!"

Soldiers came to the station that morning, but with no evil intent, and one of our teachers learned from them later that during that night they had left the village and had marched up the road to the Mission station. The soldiers, stimulated by drink, admitted they had every intention of violence upon the little family, but barring the road was an unseen Hand. They could advance no farther in spite of the smouldering hatred in their hearts. Frustrated and perplexed they returned to the village. The children slept, unmolested and undisturbed, in the safety of the hollow of His hand. God had stepped in.

HEALTH AND HOLINESS

"*With long life will I satisfy him, and shew him my salvation*" Psalm 91: 16.

FRANK CHAPMAN *Spanish Guinea*

THE work of the Worldwide Evangelization Crusade in southern Rio Muni has known the touch of the supernatural since its inception in 1933. Mr. and Mrs. Alex. Thorne pioneered the Okak field. Their presence was not at first appreciated as the priests had warned the people that Satan had come to Rio Muni in the guise of the evangelical missionary. As Mr. Thorne visited the villages, Africans fled in horror at the sight of the supposed "devils". As time went by Mr. Thorne through his medical knowledge alleviated the sufferings of the people, and saved the lives of many children. This above all convinced the Okaks that the "devil" was not such a bad person after all.

Due to the fact that hundreds of people of this Roman Catholic country were converted to Christ persecution broke upon the Okak church in the early 1950's. Eighteen of the twenty-five new chapels were destroyed; some were burned to the ground, others torn apart and plundered, and still others closed until they finally fell into disrepair. Along with this came the imprisonment of believers and evangelists for the sake of the gospel. In the Nsorc area, believers were prohibited from meeting together even in a home for prayer and fellowship. There were more trials to follow.

In 1956 there seemed to be an enemy attack upon my life as Field Leader. I became afflicted with a serious illness, terrible abscesses appearing from time to time upon my body. After a thorough medical examination at the Camerun Mission Hospital, the doctors informed me that my pancreas had ceased to function, and that I was a diabetic.

A more serious type of opposition was now encountered. It became apparent that Satan had succeeded in causing division among the believers. This attack was subtle and undercover, and was robbing the Okak church of the unity and power of the Spirit. But "the Son of God was manifested that He might destroy the works of the devil" (1 John 3: 8).

Encouragement came early in 1957. As a diabetic, I was faced with a critical situation in that dieting was almost impossible. The taking of insulin while trekking in the jungle is very dangerous. My wife and I then felt led to ask the Lord to work a miracle. Whether instantly or not, we do not know, but in May 1957 I realized that I was feeling fine, and that in spite of taking no precautions or medicine, there were no more recurrences of abscesses or infections upon my body. I then went to the coastal city of Bata and underwent a very thorough blood analysis. We received the report; my blood was in perfect condition and my pancreas was now functioning normally. What a thrill to experience the healing touch of the God of the Impossible!

With the assurance that God would step in, we gave ourselves to seek His help. It is one thing to let the enemy in, but entirely another to get him out. At this point many pastors and missionaries became discouraged, and were tempted to throw up their hands in despair. The Okak church was in dire need of revival. During the annual two-weeks' Bible Conference in the Cogo area the Lord gave the elders and myself a greater burden for prayer. Our regular Thursday afternoon prayer-meeting seemed so lacking in power; too much saying of prayers, and not real praying in the Spirit. At the close of the meeting I challenged those interested to meet with me at 9 p.m. when we would give ourselves to seek the Lord. About twelve responded, and what a wonderful time we had. The meeting lasted all through the night until the morning meeting commenced at 6 o'clock. The first thing the Lord reminded us of was that if we wanted revival in the work, we must first have revival in our own hearts. As we gave ourselves to seek the Lord, we were challenged to follow the example of David, Isaiah, and Daniel. David cried, "Search *me*, O God, and know *my* heart: try *me*, and know *my* thoughts: and see if there be any wicked way in *me*" (Psalm 139: 23, 24). Isaiah cried, "Woe is *me*! for *I* am undone; because *I* am a man of unclean lips" (Isaiah 6: 5). Daniel cried, "While I was speaking, and praying, and confessing *my* sin . . ." (Daniel 9: 20). We were shut in to the matter of one's own sin. We had to use the personal pronoun in the singular, "*I*", "*me*", or "*my*". We had no freedom to pray for anyone or anything else, until all those present had allowed the searchlight of the Holy Spirit to reveal and expose all sin. As one after another confessed and renounced their sin, the circle became complete, and we found ourselves both in the attitude and atmosphere of prayer.

At that time we learned of a mighty burden of prayer that God had given the evangelist at Adjamboge, in the Nsorc area. He had called his people to seek the Lord and to have special prayer on Friday evenings until midnight. Early in 1959, two church elders accompanied me on an extensive trek. We had gone several days' journey when we became conscious of a new power in our midst. God had at last found a favourable situation through which He could work and Himself be glorified. He found hearts that had been cleansed and melted together in the unity of the Spirit. The love of Christ had been shed abroad into our hearts by the Holy Ghost.

From April until our departure for furlough in 1959,

the Spirit of God was being poured out upon the work. Many souls came to know Christ as Saviour, and great conviction of sin came upon many others. There was weeping over sin such as we had not previously seen. Because the people sensed the power of God in our midst, they brought their sick to be anointed in the name of the Lord, according to James 5: 14. This ministry of healing has continued from time to time to this day.

In 1959 a group of us were on a motor trip to the eastern area. At Adjamboge the need for revival was great, as many had grown cold and had become indifferent to the claims of Christ. Conviction of sin came upon the whole group of about sixty souls. Confession of sin and seeking of forgiveness went on and on. In the meeting was a man who had been an evangelist but due to falling into sin, had been relieved of his position. In that meeting he confessed to have smoked opium, was a thief, and had committed adultery. He was not yet through, as again he was standing confessing more. He was constrained to confess his visits to the witch-doctor. At that moment he was seized by a tremendous power, and thrown violently to the ground in agony. He screamed and acted like a maniac. God had assured us of victory over *all* the power of the enemy, and we thus looked steadfastly to heaven, praising the Lord. He was soon delivered and regained his composure. Near midnight, another young man suddenly sprang forward and threw himself at our feet, confessing sin and desperately seeking forgiveness from the Lord. We asked him later why he had not confessed earlier in the meeting. He told us that he had wanted to but that a power had seized him and that he was frozen to his seat until the power of God triumphed. Before leaving next morning, we were detained in order that we could further help those who had been dealt with by the Holy Spirit. Some confessed that they had never been born again. When God moves by His Spirit, souls are easily dealt with.

Thus, because we accepted the challenge, God stepped in and has given a three-fold victory against the three-fold Satanic attack. *First*, the outward opposition, whether political or religious, has practically disappeared. We are now experiencing more liberty in the work than ever. There are no believers in prison. Meetings continue everywhere unmolested. Medical work has increased, and for the first time in the history of the work, we have a recognized grade school on the Mission. *Second*, the more serious problem within the ranks of the believers has been completely eliminated. Warm fellowship in the Spirit exists between the missionaries and the Africans. All the church workers, including the elders, the evangelists, and the lay preachers, are united in the bonds of the love of Christ, labouring together to make Him known among their people. *Third*, God's touch upon my body has been complete, with no recurrence of diabetes. We have become conscious of the truth of God's promise in Romans 8: 11, "If the Spirit of Him that raised up Jesus from the dead dwell in you, He that raised up Christ from the dead shall also quicken your mortal bodies by His Spirit that dwelleth in you." Though much time was given to prayer, to a lot of trekking through jungles and while suffering a serious illness, yet, at the time of our departure for furlough, we were able to depart being both physically and spiritually refreshed.

BONES, BREAD, AND BROWN SUGAR

"*The Lord had visited His people in giving them bread*"
Ruth 1: 6.

ELIZABETH ANTHONY *London Headquarters*

LITTLE did I know of all that would be involved when I stepped in to fill a gap and be responsible for the catering and cooking for the family at Headquarters. For years previously I had proved God in the life and walk of faith, yet this was a new experience and it was certainly good that I was unaware of all it meant. God continually intervened in particular ways, making the years of such joy and happiness in proving Him. We saw Him meet the smallest as well as the largest need. His timing was always perfect. His grace was plentiful. Without Him nothing could have been done and His word was strength to me.

The household purse was handed to me on Thursday and there was only sixpence in it. There was next to nothing in the cupboards! A family of over sixty to be fed, and we faced the month-end Conference with extra visitors over the weekend for meals! That was my first introduction. Somewhat dazed I went to our heavenly Father and told Him that He would have to do something or I would finish up with an ulcer! My reading the next morning was 1 Kings 17, and verse 13 stood out, "Fear not", then verse 14, "The barrel of meal shall not waste, neither shall the cruse of oil fail." That was just God's word to me and I thanked Him, and wholly trusted Him. Yet, I was still a wee bit fearful but He forgave me and from that moment until I handed back the responsibility I never experienced the same fear. He was true to His word.

Saturday was Conference day and it began with a gift of £15 out of the blue! I could not believe my eyes. I looked; I counted the notes over and over again to convince myself of the truth. This was His deliverance and His encouragement. That first big deliverance was precious.

Weeks went by and I had now taken a stand to see God deliver us in many big ways. I felt we should buy in larger quantities. I contemplated launching out in ordering a ton of potatoes and wondered where they could be got cheaply. Then I was reminded of a friend in the country who had helped in the past. I contacted him. This resulted in our obtaining potatoes regularly and cheaply, and sometimes one of the farmers would give us a ton as a gift. That always happened when we were in particular need. The farmer knew nothing of this urgency at all, but it was just our heavenly Father stepping in to make this provision. Every time they were delivered I found the cartage expenses were also paid. On some occasions the potatoes were topped up with a load of firewood or vegetables, such was their generosity.

I was introduced to a meat buyer (who was a Christian) with one of the shops near us. The following result was that on the groceries and meat we got 1*s.* 6*d.* in the £ reduction, which cut our expenses down tremendously. We even got the marrow bones added for nothing; whereas before I had to pay 1*s.* 6*d.* for such extras.

God led us on in these practical things. A large tea urn became a necessity. We prayed and waited. One day I saw just what we wanted. We got in touch with the firm and our conversation revealed they were Christians, and more than interested in the Lord's work. We made an appointment to see them. I had 3*s.* 6*d.* in the purse. That showroom whetted my appetite for all the nice kitchen equipment we could have done with. Our friend showed us two urns, one that would hold sixty cups, and the other a hundred cups. He kept saying that I would need two! My faith did not rise so high—I was thinking of the £.*s.d.* Finally I settled for the larger of the two. Then, to my surprise, he told me it was their gift to the work. I was deeply touched and moved. It was priced at £15 and to us it was a wonderful gift. We can get ninety cups out of ¼ lb. of tea. I wrote later to the gentleman expressing again our gratitude and telling him how God had led and the amount we had. He wrote back saying that that morning he and his wife had promised the Lord they would make it a gift to the work. It is wonderful to see God at work.

We saw the Lord's faithful stewards remember us in our daily need. A blind lady month by month faithfully brought her gift for the kitchen box together with string shopping bags that she made herself. Another old lady brought tins of shoe polish, cakes of toilet soap, washing powder, biscuits, rock, and chocolate for the children. Yet another called leaving three 1 lb. jars of marmalade and the same of butter and of cooking fat. Yes, we were in real need that day of these items for our missionary families. I wrote and told her what an answer to prayer it was. She wrote telling me that she was over seventy-six years of age, and used to come to our Headquarters' prayer-meetings many years before. Every week-end for many years our baker faithfully supplied us with bread, buns, cakes (cream ones as well), pies, sausage rolls, and very often brown sugar, syrup, custard powder, Christmas pudding, and Christmas cakes—all without cost.

Shall I ever forget the day the postman delivered a parcel which contained 4 lb. of cheese, all the way from Ireland. This was just in time to make macaroni cheese for dinner. Without that gift it would have been macaroni without the cheese. With what perfection of timing is the Lord's care for us.

"Uncle Hoppy" is another of God's obedient and sacrificial servants who faithfully remembers us by bringing eggs, potatoes, flour, sugar, and all our fruit for jam making. Again and again we would find everything provided to make 800 lb. of jam. One day his lorry drove up with 1 cwt. of flour, potatoes, 1 cwt. of sugar and of plums, six cases of apples, two large crates of dates, raisins, currants, and butter. I had just ordered flour at the grocers. Seeing the flour just delivered, I went back to the shop and told them to cancel the order as God had so wonderfully provided. They looked in amazement and confessed that they had forgotten to order that item! The Lord embarrasses no one in His planning.

An old friend, not seen for years, rang me up just before Christmas. I could not believe my ears when I heard him ask, "Could you do with three large turkeys weighing 28 lb. each, 336 eggs, and two gallons of cream?" Our Christmas dinner was provided for! I could hardly keep my feet still for joy at God's goodness. He had stepped in and provided abundantly again. But that is not all. The same day at the door was delivered another turkey and 4 lb. of butter, tins of fruit, chocolate, coconut ice, and jellies. These were wonderful "extras" from God.

At times the shopkeepers were touched by God to sell goods at half price, and sometimes sent without any charge. Their generosity towards us was beyond description. Harvest Festival gifts, too, came to us through the goodness and kind thought of the Lord's people. These gifts have been such a help in varying the diet.

These are but a few of the thrilling instances of seeing God meet our needs and fulfil His word, "Blessed shall be thy basket and thy store." Yes, there have also been the days of scarcity as well as of plenty, but we have walked thankfully with God. He has always provided and although sometimes things have been somewhat meagre, yet we have never been without a meal.

From shoelaces to thousands of pounds have been the gifts to meet repairs and decorating, cleaning and laundry bills, baker's and milk accounts. The latter have all been met day to day and we have been able to praise God that we owe no man anything!

OUR ASSURANCE POLICY

"I will answer him . . . I will honour him"
Psalm 91:15.

LEN MOULES *W.E.C. Headquarters, London*

It is a regular custom in all our Home Bases that each morning we gather for a time around the Word. Projects are shared and prayed over. The mind of the Lord is sought regarding ventures. Prayer targets are gripped in intercession and with importunity based on the promises of God.

Through the years of mission history we have seen difficulties yield to prayer. We have also seen the difficulties change shape. Visas for foreign lands were not always hard to obtain, but now they often call for prayer and faith. Not so long ago eight visas were required for three different countries. Candidates and Staff were on their knees together pleading and prevailing in prayer. All eight came through within one week! Praise God.

Countless are the occasions upon which equipment, finances, and properties have been supplied in time and from donors completely unaware of the need. These requirements are known only to the W.E.C. "family" of full-time workers. Here is a typical occasion of God faithfully stepping in to meet a need.

The missionaries of the Crusade move to their Field without any *human* guarantee of financial support. There is no assured salary for them, nor a promised furlough at pre-determined periods. They accept a personal assurance from the Word, "God your Father knoweth what things ye have need of" (Matt. 6: 8, R.V. margin). This in no wise releases a Home Base from responsibility in these matters, for God has taught us deeply the meaning of fellowship. This is not merely lip-service, but a vital identification with others in their need and a willingness to be the possible channels of supply.

One mid-month the money for Allowances was very low. The Treasurer passed a message about this to the leader of the morning prayer session. Unitedly we asked the Lord for the finance required to maintain the Crusade overseas. A week passed with no appreciable gift to answer our call. It was now a real challenge which we accepted. We gathered for a half-night on our knees. It was a time of unusual freedom in prayer and faith as we revelled in the realization of God's authority in this through the Holy Spirit. We rose from our knees knowing that God had heard.

Eagerly we awaited the handsome donation which must now come to complete the account. A week followed without a deliverance. Puzzled and confused we sent the money we had to the fields. Only half the usual amounts were dispatched. I was baffled, and felt I ought to send a personal letter to each field expressing our regret at the low Allowance, and explain the prayer we maintained and assurance God had given us—yet without any visible result.

Some time later replies were received. There was a unanimity in their testimony that they looked to God, and to Him alone, to meet every possible need, yet how deeply grateful they were for the exercise of fellowship the Home Base was maintaining with them. Then followed accounts of the diverse ways in which God had provided.

A year previously Colombia had received a larger sum than usual from the Home Base, and had put the balance to one side for a future necessity. God had confirmed to them that this was the necessity. The balance equalled the deficit.

Senegal testified to receiving full financial income that month. An unexpected gift from France filled the gap in Allowances that we had regretted.

We knew that the hardest hit by any deficit would be a Field with few missionaries. At this time the Canary Islands had only one lady worker. Our concern for her was the greater. Then came her testimony how she had been travelling between the Islands and had stayed overnight with missionary friends. They had not previously given any financial gift to the work, but as she was leaving on this occasion they shared that the thought had been impressed upon them that they should give her their tithe. The tithe equalled the deficit! So God, in various and wonderful ways, stepped in to fulfil His assurance to us that every need would be met.

This is not the unusual. It is the day-to-day experience of those of us in the Crusade who look only to Him, and live from His hand to our mouth. Wonderful is our Lord's concern for each of us.

VISIONS OF A VISA

"*And the government shall be upon His shoulder*"
Isaiah 9: 6.

BESSIE BRIERLEY *Portuguese Guinea*

AFTER eighteen months' work in Portuguese Guinea sixteen souls were saved and on my departure the little flock was left alone. The door of their meeting-place was closed, and they were forbidden to gather for further services.

It was said in Government circles that their missionary would never return. It seemed to prove true, for every effort to get visas on our passports had failed. After long waiting, Leslie, my husband, and I finally returned to Senegal and to a W.E.C. station just north of the Portuguese Guinea frontier.

From there Leslie took the very long journey to Dakar to try and get in touch with the Portuguese Consul. He even paid £12 for a telegram to Portuguese Guinea applying again for our visa. It was all in vain.

It meant everything to us to get back to that little group. One day while praying, the Lord impressed me to go over the border and see the Governor of Guinea. I came out and told my husband. "Bessie," said Leslie, when I told him, "I could not tell you to do this, but if God has told you then you must obey."

Mr. and Mrs. Barron offered to look after our child, Norman, then only two years old. The French Commandant gave the pass to travel to the frontier, and even offered to take me there in his car.

Leslie accompanied me to the frontier, but then he had to return. "Leslie, what shall I say to the officials when I meet them?" I asked, almost in tears. "The Lord will tell you what to say," he replied.

On crossing the frontier I could only find a trader, and he kindly offered to put me up. He said cars were running all the time, and one would take me on south to Bissau. But five days passed and no car came through. What a test of faith! How the enemy taunted me, "Go back; you will close the door to Portuguese Guinea for ever in this illegal entry." I was reading in the book of Esther, and it seemed as though it was written for me. It was not legal for her to go to the king, but she went and her petition was granted. On the fifth day a lorry appeared and I obtained a lift to the first town with an Administration Post. After much prayer I went up to see the Administrator. "Sir, I have been in Portuguese Colonies previously for six years and I want now to go to Bissau. Will you give me permission?" "Have you a passport?" he asked. "Yes," I said, handing him a new passport with not even an old visa on it. He looked through it carefully. I believe

God made him to see visas on every page! "Yes, you may go right ahead," was his decision. I went down the road shouting Hallelujah!

I arrived in Bissau and asked for an appointment with the Governor, and found to my amazement that a *new* man had been appointed a few weeks before my arrival. This was a wonderful answer to prayer! The day before my interview with the Governor I gathered our little group of believers together. We worshipped and wept together. "Brothers, if you want us to come back to Guinea, you must ask God to give us visas. Let us pray and fast tomorrow until I go to see His Excellency the Governor." This we did. The Governor received me well, but said he would have to refer my affairs to Lisbon. I asked, "Sir, will you allow me to stay in Guinea till the matter is resolved." After a moment's consideration he gave the verdict. "Well, you know, er, well, all right; you may stay."

Six weeks slowly passed. No visas were granted, and now the rains were approaching. My family were many miles away in Senegal. How I longed for them, but how much I also wanted the visas. I paid another visit to the Governor, with no resulting satisfaction. I paced the floor of my room pleading with God for the visas.

One day a young convert, a telegraph boy, said, "Señhora, I'm sure you're going to get the visas. Last night the Lord told me in a dream." A few days later another of those simple believers in Christ said he also had had a dream in which the visas had been granted. Then came the fulfilment of visions. A day or two later I was called to the Governor's office to collect visas for three British subjects. God had heard our cry. Hallelujah!

It was a combined operation. Leslie had been wrestling with God, and when he had got the assurance of faith, wrote on a small piece of paper which is precious to us yet, "I believe God will give the visas. He will open Bissau, Bolama, Balanta country, and the Bijagos Islands. Signed, L. Brierley." "Faith without works is dead" is the directive of God's word, so he packed our trunks and stacked them ready to go on the lorry. Every night he prayed with Norman, who was then just lisping his first prayers after Daddy; "Dear God, send Mummy back quickly with sweets, shoes, cheese, and visas."

God stepped in and supplied them all, and we entered Portuguese Guinea again to continue our missionary work of evangelism and leprosy treatment.

Some years later a Government doctor threatened to close down the leprosy work. In angry tones he said, "In fifteen days I will close down this work." About the end of that period a guard appeared at the door. "Señhor Brierley, the head doctor wants to see you in town." We gasped. "Is he now going to fulfil his threat?" My husband prepared to go while the rest of the missionaries got down on their knees and prayed, "Oh Lord, don't close down the leprosy work." (All our missionaries at that time had come out under the leprosy scheme, except my husband and me. If the leprosy work were closed they also might have to leave.)

Leslie entered the doctor's office and was told to be seated. In a gruff voice the doctor said, "Mr. Brierley, a baby has been born in the leprosy camp. I don't want it there a moment longer than is necessary. Would you be willing to take it to the Mission?" (No baby is born with leprosy even though both parents may have the disease.) My husband gasped, "Er . . . Yes, all right; we'll take it!"

When Leslie returned we got up from our knees wide-eyed and fearful and asked, "What is it?" "Bessie, get your things on quickly; the doctor wants us to take a baby born just a few hours ago, into our home." "A baby?" I queried. "Yes, a baby!"

We collected a shawl and got into the doctor's car. He told me, on the way to the Camp, that the first time he took a baby from its mother the woman tore his shirt off his back. I prayed much in that car. "Oh Lord, give the mother grace to let me have that baby."

The mother knew us immediately we entered the ward. Our nurses had gone regularly to that Camp and had taught those women about Jesus. They had learnt to understand the Scriptures and to sing choruses.

Those mutilated hands had learnt to sew. I began quietly to plead with that dear mother, "You don't want your baby to live in this Camp all her life, do you? Surely you don't want her to get leprosy, do you?" She sadly shook her head. I held out my arms in love asking, "Won't you give that baby to me? I'll love her and bring her back as many times as I can for you to see." The mother quietly took the baby from beside her and handed her to me without showing a tear. I was nearly overcome, choking with a lump in my throat.

We called the baby "Elizabeth" after our Queen in England. She *was* a little queen.

A baby changed that antagonistic doctor to become our best friend, but the price was high! Every time a baby was born at the Government leprosy camp a guard appeared and said, "Señhora, another baby!" We have eleven from that Camp, and twenty-three in all, but praise God the work goes on in Portuguese Guinea. God stepped in again—through a babe.

WORLDWIDE EVANGELIZATION CRUSADE

FIELDS

Arabia
Brazil
Canary Islands
Chad
Colombia
Dominica
France
Gambia
Ghana
India
Indonesia
Iran
Italy
Ivory Coast
Japan
Korea
Liberia
Nepal
Pakistan
Portuguese Guinea
Senegal
Singapore
Spain
Taiwan
Thailand
Upper Volta
Uruguay
Venezuela
Viet Nam
Zaire (Congo)

GENERAL HEADQUARTERS

Britain
Bulstrode, Gerrards Cross, Bucks. SL9 8SZ

S. Africa
8 Sutton Crescent, Durban, Natal

N. America
Box A, Fort Washington, Pa. 19034, U.S.A.

Australia
48 Woodside Avenue, Strathfield, Sydney, N.S.W. 2135

Germany
WEK-Missionshaus, D-6239 Vockenhausen/Ts.

Holland
Dunanstraat 30b, Rotterdam-6

New Zealand
15 Henley Road, Mt. Eden, Auckland 3

Scandinavia
Morkullegatan 50, S-724 69 Vasteras, Sweden

Switzerland
Hochstrasse 132, CH 8330 Pfaffikon/ZH